Legal Almanac Series No. 70

THE LAW AND LEGISLATION OF CREDIT CARDS:
Use and Misuse

by IRVING J. SLOAN

Irving J. Sloan
General Editor

1987
Oceana Publications, Inc.
London • Rome • New York

Library of Congress Catalog Card Number: 86-063542
ISBN: 0-379-11158-6

© Copyright 1987 by Oceana Publications, Inc.

Manufactured in the United States of America

TABLE OF CONTENTS

"Who steals my purse steals trash" is not true anymore. If your purse is full of credit cards he steals money *and* your good name.

Joey Adams Encyclopedia of Humor

INTRODUCTION

"All of a sudden, the credit card was like an Aladdin's lamp and you didn't even have to rub it." These words, expressing something more akin to pride than to remorse, were offered by a nineteen-year-old boy in explanation of a one month trip back and forth across the country. During his escapade, the boy purchased nearly ten thousand dollars' worth of goods and services by the simple expedient of making frequent and extravagant use of his credit card. The omnipotent credit card was used to obtain rental cars, airline tickets, luxurious hotel suites, food and drink, clothing, a mink coat for a newly-acquired girl friend, and a dog for himself. This brief case history reported in the press recently bears out the fact that credit cards can be used to buy almost any conceivable item or service. It also indicates that credit cards are subject to serious abuse and that the potential liabilities of the credit card issuer, credit card holder, and honoring merchant are not hypothetical or trivial, but very real and very substantial.

Clearly one of the most important commercial developments since the Second World War is the emergence of the credit card as a substitute for cash. While it appears that losses due to improper or fraudulent use of credit cards is negligible compared to the overall volume of use, there have been some startling examples of individuals who have stolen thousands of dollars through fraudulent use of credit cards, and losses have increased as a result of the inability of users to meet their financial obligations. As the reader will see from a review of the Appendix A in this volume, the general criminal statutes of the various states relating to larceny and forgery seem to cover most of the more flagrant misuses of credit cards. In addition, again as seen in the statutes reproduced in Appendix A,

1

many states have enacted statutes imposing criminal penalties for specified improper uses. Increasingly, a large number of states have enacted special legislation dealing with the use and misuse of credit cards. This legislation, as the reader will note in our Appendix A, comes under titles such as "Credit Card Fraud Act" (Arizona), "Credit Card Crimes" (Connecticut), "Illegal Use of Financial Transaction Cards" (Georgia), "Credit Card Number Protection Act" (Maryland), and "Financial Transaction Card Crime Act" (North Carolina).

History of the Credit Card

Since the beginning of history man has been involved with trade and commerce. As this area has expanded and become more important, different mediums of exchange have been developed. Barter gave way to the advance of money, and money in turn has faced the advance of checks. Now both are feeling the advance of credit cards. In this age of rapid technological advances it is only natural that man should seek out a new, more efficient system of carrying on trade and commerce. This system seems to be the credit card.

Again, credit cards are not new. They, or some equivalent, have existed since the early part of this century. Some time before 1920 some large department stores began to issue "credit coins." These coins were a small piece of metal which displayed the name of the merchant and a series of numbers identifying the customer's account. These coins were issued to good customers and allowed them to purchase merchandise on credit in the store. About the same time, oil companies began to issue charge plates (usually made of metal) to their customers for the purchase of gasoline, oil, etc. at the companies' service stations. All of this development notwithstanding, the yield was relatively insignificant until 1950.

In 1950, the Diners' Club, Inc. introduced the first independent credit card plan. This plan involved an agreement between the club and its members and between the club and the merchants. The members agreed to pay the club to obtain a card and then agreed to pay each monthly billing as it came in. The merchant agreed to honor the card and then forward his credit vouchers to Diners' Club for payment once a month. The members thereby were able to get service from many types of establishments by carrying only one card and were able to pay for it at the end of the month. The merchant, on the other hand, was relieved of having to have his own plan and was also likely to increase the volume of his business since card holding members would find it more convenient to deal with him than with a merchant who wouldn't honor his card. The success of the Diners' Club plan was such that the American Express Company entered the field in 1958, while Hilton Credit Corporation initiated the "Carte Blanche" plan the following year.

In 1951, the First National Bank of Long Island became the first bank to offer its customers a credit card plan. This area was not very important, however, until the late 1950s when the Bank of America and the Chase Manhattan Bank issued their cards. In 1966, the Midwest Bank Card System was started.

With the advent of the bank credit card the range of goods and services available on credit became staggering. They range from the normal expenditures of food and clothing, shelter, entertainment and travel.

By at least the beginnings of the 1970s the personal (as well as the corporate) credit card had become a fixture in the nation's economy. Today more than 60 million credit card accounts exist in the United States, and seven out of

3

ten households possess at least one credit card. By 1986 outstanding balances on credit card accounts total more than $80 billion.

The law and legislation relating to credit cards is essentially in an embryonic condition. However, statutory treatment codifying the law related to credit cards has increased in recent years. This development will, hopefully, avoid the problem of forcing the credit card into an existing legal mold in which it does not quite fit. The statutory treatment offers the advantages of removing much of the uncertainty which has greatly characterized the "law" of credit cards until very recently. The statutes serve as guidelines both for commercial practices and court decisions. Because the statutes play such a crucial role in this field, our appendixes are fairly comprehensive in the inclusion of both state and federal statutes.

In short, what we have here is an evolving commercial system, the cashless society not so much of the future but already in our present.

Chapter 1

THE MECHANICS AND ECONOMIC CHARACTERISTICS OF CREDIT CARD PLANS

Mechanics

Credit card plans involve one card issuer and many merchants and card holders. Because the form contracts used are drafted by the issuer and because only one merchant and one card holder are involved in a particular credit card transaction, it is appropriate to consider the plans as three-party arrangements, referring to all merchants as "the merchant" and to all card holders as "the card holder." The issuer is the moving force of the plan, and the success of its endeavor is dependent upon the solicitation of both merchants and retail buyers.

The issuer distributes credit cards upon application. In the early years of the credit card movement card issuers mailed unsolicited credit cards to individuals whose names had been taken from mass-mailing lists. Large quantities of these credit cards were stolen in the postal system and from recipients' mailboxes without the knowledge of the individual to whom the unsolicited card had been sent. In 1970, Congress curbed such practices by amending the Truth in Lending Act to provide for regulation of the credit card industry. An absolute ban on the unsolicited distribution of credit cards presently exists in the law.

The credit card holder is entitled to purchase goods and services at any retail outlet which has become a merchant member of the plan. For this privilege, the card holder is to pay the issuer for "all credit extended on the basis of this card" or for "all purchases made with the card" until the issuer receives written notice of the loss or theft of the card.

5

At the end of each billing period, the issuer consolidates all of the purchases made by the card holder from merchant members during the period and sends him one all-inclusive statement. Under the consumer plans, upon receipt of each monthly statement the holder has the option of paying the face amount of the bill within a specified period, usually twenty-five to thirty days from the date the statement is mailed, or of paying according to a deferred payment schedule. On the other hand, credit cards held by business people as distinguished from retail purchasers of consumer goods, usually have no such option, nor do they pay a service charge. The sole cost imposed upon such credit card holders is the annual fee. Upon receipt of their statement, they are expected promptly to pay their bill in full.

If the consumer credit card holder selects the deferred payment plan, he must pay a certain percentage of the total bill within twenty-five to thirty days, depending upon the particular plan. The remainder is paid in monthly installments and is subject to a service charge which is essentially interest which is computed each month at a specified percentage of the previous month's balance less all appropriate credits.

At the time of the customer's application for a credit card, he is given a maximum amount of credit. At any given time the credit available to him is dependent upon the amount owing to the issuer. This is known as a "revolving credit" feature.

The rights and duties of the merchant member of the plan are contained in a form contract drafted by the issuer. He is obligated to "assign" or "endorse" to the issuer all "sales drafts," "charge slips," or "accounts," which represent sales made to card holders (see Chapter 3 for the legal implications of this). With certain exceptions, the issuer's "purchase" of sales drafts or accounts is "without recourse' to the merchant in the event of nonpayment by card holders.

These exceptions are defined in some of the form contracts in vague and uncertain terms for the issuer's own protection. But generally it can be said that the issuer will have recourse to the merchant (meaning the issuer can hold the merchant liable for a card holder's nonpayment) when the face of the card indicates that it has expired; when the card is on the current void list sent by the issuer to the merchant; when the sales slip is illegible or not signed by the person who made the purchase; when there is non-delivery of merchandise; when there is a breach of warranty or fraudulent acts on the part of the merchant; or when the merchant, without prior clearance from the issuer, allows the card holder to make a purchase in excess of the single-purchase limit established by the issuer. In other words, in those situations where the conduct of the merchant is responsible for improper validation of the purchase, the issuer may hold the merchant liable.

In addition to assuming the credit risk (apart from the above litany of exceptions), the issuer handles the billing procedures, makes all collections from card holders, and investigates the credit rating of card applicants. The issuer's compensation for these services is obtained by discounting the sales drafts assigned to it by the merchant at a rate established by the contract.

What has thus far been described is the *three-party* credit card which has become pretty much the prevailing credit card transaction. But the original *two-party* credit card arrangement remains popular and its operation should at least be briefly described here.

In the *two-party* credit card transaction—exemplified by the department store credit card or plate—the customer agrees to pay for his credit purchase in one lump sum at the next regular billing date, or he may place his charges on a revolving line of credit basis. There may be a combination of these payment plans. These credit cards are then used by the customer in making purchases at the store of the issuer and the store's salesperson may be required to ascertain if the purchase is within the limit of credit set by the store for this particular customer. While this was once carried out by telephone today the system is computerized and a computer next to every cash register conveys the information within seconds.

A newer development in the use of credit cards has been to obtain cash or a line of credit. Most banks have issued credit cards which enable the holder to secure an installment loan from the bank, to cash bank checks (which resemble a hybrid of postal money order and a cashier's check) and to overdraw his checking account and cover it by a loan.

Economic Characteristics

Gasoline Company Credit Cards

Gasoline credit cards are "two-party," arrangements—credit cards that are issued by a merchant or vendor for customers to use in making credit purchases primarily or exclusively at the retail outlets of the issuing company. Most gasoline company credit card programs provide credit for a one-month billing period with no provision for extending repayment over a longer period. Some gasoline companies offer optional extended periods to pay for purchases of more expensive items such as tires, batteries, or repairs.

As a result of the short repayment period, the gross expense to the gasoline companies of financing these receivables is lower, relative to the dollar volume of credit billings, than for credit card programs that offer extended

8

repayment terms. However, an offsetting factor is the relatively low amount of finance charge revenue generated by this type of credit card plan. Moreover, the rather low average amount of credit purchases at gasoline stations implies that costs of processing credit card transactions tend to be fairly high per dollar credit of sales.

Since publication of this volume, Congress has passed legislation which requires gasoline stations to offer consumers a choice between purchasing their products and services either at a discount if they pay cash or with a credit card. This requirement removes the burden of both higher prices and service charges for credit card holders.

Bank Credit Cards

By contrast, bank credit cards are, again, "third party" arrangements in which the company that provides the financial service has no affiliation with the buyer or seller of the goods and services purchased with the credit card. Bank credit cards offer highly flexible credit terms. Customers who can qualify for a fairly large credit limit-those who have a good credit history and adequate income can incur relatively large indebtedness on such an account. Also, by choosing to pay less than the entire balance, account holders can stretch out repayments over an extended period of time. Bank credit cards can therefore be used to satisfy fairly large needs for immediate credit, and, if desired, to scale repayments to available income. Furthermore, bank credit cards are widely accepted for purchases of a large variety of goods and services, and can also be used to obtain cash at many financial institutions, as indicated earlier.

The gross financing cost incurred by a typical bank credit card issuer per dollar of credit billings likely exceeds that of most gasoline credit card programs, since a lower proportion of bank credit card customers usually pay the entire balance when billed. Processing costs are lower relative to the volume of bank credit card billings because of the larger average dollar amount of bank credit transactions.

Although the term "bank" credit card is commonly used, it obscures the growing diversity of institutions and organizations offering such services. "Bank" cards now are issued by finance companies (through commercial banks that may be subsidiaries), savings and loan associations, and credit unions. Some nonfinancial organizations such as the American Automobile Association (AAA) have made arrangements with commercial banks to issue bank credit cards to members in the name of the organization.

To offset the cost pressures, many banks have adopted periodic fees in an effort to boost their revenues and to reprice credit card services on a basis better suited to an environment in which customer deposit rates are unrestricted. Some banks have pursued means of boosting revenues other than through imposing periodic fees, such as charging for each transaction billed to a credit card account and assessing penalties for late payments, for replacement of lost cards, or for balances that exceed credit limits.

A variant of the bank credit card offered by many institutions is the so-called "gold card" or the "premium card." This specialized type of "premium" bank credit card combines the features of the regular bank credit card with a larger credit line and a package of additional services that may include accident insurance, lost credit card service, hotel and car rental discounts, and free travelers checks. Fees charged cardholders for gold card services usually are greater than the range of fees on regular bank credit card accounts, but ordinarily are less than the fees charged for general purposes (travel and entertainment) cards.

One-half of all families in the United States now hold one or more bank credit cards, up from nearly two-fifths in 1977. The proportion of families holding a bank credit card has expanded continually, as has the percentage of families that use bank credit cards, which rose from one-fifth in 1971 to somewhat more than one-half in 1982.

General Purpose Credit Cards

These credit cards are also frequently referred to as "travel and entertainment cards." Major issuers of such cards include American Express, Carte Blanche, and Diner's Club.

Also frequently referred to as "travel and entertainment cards," this type of third-party credit card is oriented toward more affluent customers able to pay a larger annual membership fee for access to premium credit card services. Since higher income requirements must be met to qualify for general purpose credit cards, an element of prestige may be attached to carrying such cards as well as some presumption that cardholder credit worthiness is less subject to question than with other credit cards. Therefore, these programs appeal to customers who travel and/or entertain frequently, for whom an easily accepted credit card with a relatively high credit limit can be especially convenient.

A variety of ancillary services is typically offered as part of a general purpose credit card package. Travel accident insurance, discounts on travelers checks, on hotel accommodations, and on car rental, and access to check cashing or cash advances from company or affiliated offices or from card-activated cash dispensers are examples of these additional services.

In addition to membership fees, card issuers also derive revenues from merchant discount charges paid by retailers. Another important feature of general purpose credit cards is the requirement that balances be repaid within 30 days after billing. Thus, although the average balance for such accounts may be large, credit remains outstanding for only a relatively short period of time, so that gross financing costs incurred by the card issuers are kept fairly low in relation to the volume of billings.

General purpose credit cards are held by almost 15 percent of families, up from only eight percent in 1977. The percentage of families using general purpose credit cards has almost doubled since 1977.

Retail Store Credit Cards

Two-party credit cards issued by retail stores are the most widely held and used type of credit card. Over three-fifths of families in the United States held some kind of retail store credit card in late 1982. One can readily assume that this figure has since increased by the year of copyright of this volume. Holding and use of retail store cards have continued to expand in recent years, even though retail credit cards have long been available and despite increasing competition from third-party credit cards, some of which are now accepted by many leading department stores and specialty shops.

Retail store cards typically offer lower credit limits and have less demanding credit qualification requirements in comparison with third-party credit cards. Of course, use of retail credit cards is limited to the variety of merchandise carried by the issuing merchant. Retail revolving credit plans usually provide customers the option of repaying over an extended period of time. Typically, three-fifths of retail credit card customers usually pay the

12

entire balance billed to their accounts, about the same proportion of nonrevolvers as is found with bank credit cards. (see Appendix D.)

Other Credit Cards

The remaining category of credit cards used by consumers is highly specialized and appears to be growing slowly. Such credit cards mainly are issued by some airlines and car-rental firms.

The larger car-rental firms offer credit card accounts that have no annual fees and require full payment by the end of each billing period. Some companies provide credit card accounts only for businesses. A number of major airlines provide credit card plans that are available to individuals, permit extended payments, and have no periodic fees. In addition, many carriers accept Universal Air Travel Plan credit cards, although this account is mainly available for business travel and requires full payment during each billing period.

Chapter 2

UNAUTHORIZED USE OF CREDIT CARDS:
CIVIL ACTION

"Assuming the defendant were to have lost some currency, he, alone bears the risk of loss, and his loss is fixed by the amount of currency he lost. Should he, however, lose his credit card, the amount of loss would not be fixed, and the risk of loss is not only borne by him, but also by the Company when he actually complies with the conditions of the issuance of the card to him." *Texaco, Inc.* v. *Goldstein,* 229 N.Y.S. 2d 51, 55 (N.Y. City Mun. Ct. 1962).

The Great Credit Card Society of the 80's has come a long way since the modest department store charge plate society of earlier years. The cashless customer in the department store who used and still uses his credit card or charge plate to purchase goods on a revolving credit line has come full circle: he now uses one credit card to make purchases in almost anything almost everywhere in the country and even in the world. Beyond that he now uses credit cards to obtain cash. The pun that "cash is a poor man's credit card" has much validity today.

In addition to the obvious danger of the unwise use of credit cards by the holder resulting in debts that he is unable to pay, there is the less obvious danger that a thief or finder may impersonate the holder and use his card to incur charges which will be assessed against the holder. Virtually all credit cards attempt to shift the risk of unauthorized purchases to the holder until he gives the issuer written notice of the loss or theft of the card. This risk shifting process goes through three stages in the three-party credit card arrangement. The card holder is supposed (in the view of the issuer) to bear the risk of loss for all purchases made by an imposter between the date of loss of the card and the time that written notice is received

15

by the appropriate office of the issuer. The issuer then bears the risk of loss between this date and the date that it gives written notice to all of its affiliated merchants, hotels, restaurants, et al. The risk of loss than passes to the affiliated merchant if it should honor a credit card after it has been notified that the card has been cancelled because it was lost or stolen.

In the two-party arrangement, the risk of loss shifting prices is abbreviated: The risk of loss is on the holder until he gives written notice of the loss of the card, and since the issuer and the honoring store are the same, there should be no loss falling on the issuer.

As recently as the early 70's there were few reported cases involving suits by the issuers of credit cards against the holders for charges incurred by unauthorized users. Legislative attention to the holder's liability for the unauthorized use of this credit card was also relatively scanty. Since, however, the late 70's and continuing into the present decade there has been a virtual explosion of both federal and state legislation dealing with credit cards in general and the area of misuse in particular. Indeed, the reader will note that most of the laws presented in Appendix A focus on criminal use of credit cards than any other aspect of this developing field of the law.

In 1968, Congress enacted the Truth in Lending Act for the express purpose of "assuring a meaningful disclosure of credit terms so that the consumer will be able to compare more readily the various credit terms available to him and avoid the uninformed use of credit." Congress determined that informed use of credit would enhance economic stabilization and strengthen the competition among those financial institutions engaged in the extension of consumer credit. The Act defines consumer credit as credit extended to a natural person primarily for personal, family, household, or agricultural purposes.

The primary provisions of the 1968 Act require disclosure of credit terms in a variety of consumer credit transactions. Procedures for enforcement and liability for violations ensure compliance with those disclosure requirements.

Because the 1968 Truth in Lending Act was designed as a consumer protection statute, credit transactions involving extensions of credit for business or commercial purposes, or to governmental agencies, were exempted from coverage of the Act. Congress considered commercial and governmental debtors capable of making informed judgments as to the value of alternative credit plans, and of negotiating beneficial credit terms, so as not to require the special disclosure protection provided by the Act.

The original Truth in Lending Act did not provide any specific regulation of the growing credit card industry. As a matter of fact, the credit card industry remained largely unregulated until the late 1960s. But by the mid-1960s the credit industry had become sufficiently lucrative to create competitive practices which prompted congressional concern. Among the techniques used by credit card issuers to get quick access to broad markets was the mailing of unsolicited credit cards to individuals whose names had been taken from mass-mailing lists. Large quantities of these credit cards were stolen in the postal system and from recipients' mailboxes without the knowledge of the individual to whom the unsolicited card had been sent. In 1970, Congress attempted to curb such practices by amending the Truth in Lending Act to provide for regulation of the credit card industry. (see Appendix B.)

Early bills aimed at prohibiting unsolicited mailings of credit cards were proposed which would have given the Postal Service the authority to adopt regulations to increase security in the handling of unsolicited cards.

Eventually a bill was proposed which would have given the Federal Reserve Board authority to formulate "minimum standards to be followed by all card issuers in checking the worthiness of prospective cardholders." The Board of Governors of the Federal Reserve Board balked at assuming additional responsibilities in the area of consumer protection, and Congress amended the bill to impose an absolute ban on the unsolicited distribution of credit cards and enacted the bill as an amendment to the Truth in Lending Act. Among other things, the 1970 amendments now prohibit the issuance of unsolicited credit cards. (see Appendix B.)

The prohibition against unsolicited cards was intended to increase consumer awareness by ensuring that consumers were given adequate information regarding their rights and obligations, and to make credit card issuers more responsible in the distribution of their credit cards.

Some states began to enact legislation to limit cardholder liability for unauthorized use. One approach allowed the issuer to enforce the notice clause only if the cardholder requested the card or used it after receiving it if it was an unsolicited card. Another approach held the cardholder liable only if he did not take reasonable steps to discover the possibility of unauthorized use or did not give notice within a reasonable time after discovering the loss or theft. A number of states had no applicable statute.

Those confusing judicial and statutory approaches to limiting cardholder liability reflected basic dissatisfaction with unlimited liability for unauthorized use. Congress decided to act to ensure uniformity and to allocate more fairly the burden of loss between card issuers and cardholders. The resulting TILA (Truth in Lending Act) amendment, in addition to prohibiting mailing and issuing unsolicited credit cards, virtually eliminated cardholder liability for the unauthorized use of credit cards.

The TILA now also provides that the holder of a credit card is liable for its unauthorized use only if the card is an accepted card, and only to the extent of $50. Furthermore, the card issuer must give adequate notice to the cardholder of the potential liability, and must provide the cardholder with a self-addressed, prestamped notification to be mailed by the cardholder in the event of the loss or theft of the credit card, and the unauthorized use of the credit card must occur before the cardholder has notified the card issuer that an unauthorized use of the credit card has occurred or may occur as the result of loss, theft, or otherwise. The card issuer is also required to provide a method whereby the user of such card can be identified as the person authorized to use it. For the purposes of determining whether the card issuer has been properly notified, a cardholder notifies a card issuer by taking such steps as may be reasonably required in the ordinary course of business to provide the card issuer with the pertinent information whether or not the card issuer received such information.

In any action by a card issuer to enforce liability for the use of a credit card, the burden of proof is on the card issuer to show that the use was authorized, or that the conditions of liability for the unauthorized use have been met. Finally, these provisions do not impose on a cardholder for the unauthorized use of a credit card beyond his liability for such use under other applicable law or under any agreement with the card issuer.

It should be noted that the TILA $50 limit where the credit card has been unauthorized applies to all credit card holders, including corporations as well as individuals.

This provision is not applicable in a situation where a cardholder voluntarily and knowingly allows another person to use his credit card and that other person subsequently misuses the card. Unauthorized use of a credit card occurs only where there is no actual, implied, or apparent authority for such use by the cardholder.

The problem or the issue is understanding what is meant by "unauthorized use." The TILA itself defines unauthorized use as "use by a person other than the cardholder who does not have actual, implied or apparent authority for such use, and from which the cardholder receives no benefit." This definition focuses on the meaning of *actual, implied, or apparent authority.* The Statute does not define these terms. It now appears that the statement of the Federal Reserve Board, which is charged with interpreting the TILA and its regulations, that whether actual, implied or apparent authority exists is to be determined under state or other applicable law is all the help we have in dealing with this question.

While it is clear that unauthorized use of another's credit card by a finder or a thief is the intention and meaning of the statute, it is less clear whether unauthorized use includes use by another who initially was authorized, but whom the cardholder no longer authorizes to use the credit card. One court flatly stated:

> We hold that in instances where a cardholder, who is under no compulsion by fraud, duress or otherwise, voluntarily permits the use of his (or her) credit card by another person, the cardholder has authorized the use of that card and is thereby responsible for any charges as a result of that use.

> *Martin v. American Express, Inc.,*
> 361 So. 2d 597 (Ala. Civ. App. 1978)

On the other hand, the Federal Trade Commission, invoking the TILA, ordered a card issuer to limit the

20

liability of certain cardholders for charges made by persons whom those cardholders had voluntarily permitted to use their credit cards.

There is at the present time considerable confusion and inconsistency for resolving the cases dealing with the meaning of unauthorized use.

A Utah case of fairly recent origin in 1984 points up the present prevailing unpredictability. It is worth setting forth the facts and the reasoning in this case prototype of what is happening and can happen in this field of law.

In *Walker Bank & Trust Co. v. Jones,* the plaintiff bank tried to recover charges incurred by the separated husband of the bank's customer, Mrs. Jones. Mrs. Jones claimed the violations of the TILA absolved her of liability and rendered the bank liable for her husband's charges.

Mrs. Jones established Visa and Master Charge accounts with the bank in 1977. At her request, the bank issued credit cards on those accounts to Mrs. Jones and her husband in each of their names. Parenthetically, the reader should note here that although Mrs. Jones' husband received a credit card in his own name, he was not a "cardholder." A cardholder is "any person to whom a credit card is issued or any person who has agreed with the card issuer to pay obligations arising from the issuance of a credit card to another person." So reads the TILA statutory provision. An interpretation of this TILA section by the Federal Reserve Board, the agency charged with applying the TILA, clarifies Mr. Jones status: Where one spouse opens a "family account," only that spouse is considered a "cardholder," regardless of the names in which the cards are issued.

In November of 1977, Mrs. Jones wrote the bank two letters indicating that she would no longer honor her estranged husband's charges on those accounts. In pursuance to a clause in the cardholder agreement, the bank thereupon revoked the accounts and requested the return of all the credit cards. Both Mrs. Jones and her husband retained their cards, however, and continued to make charges against the accounts. The cards were not returned until March of 1978. By then the balance on the accounts was $2685.70, which the bank sued to recover.

The only issue before the Utah Supreme Court was whether Mrs. Jones was entitled to the protections of the TILA for her husband's use of the credit cards. In a split 3-2 decision, the court affirmed the lower district court's summary judgment for the bank and held that Mrs. Jones' husband's use of the credit card was not "unauthorized" within the meaning of the TILA. The protections of that law did not apply and Mrs. Jones was liable under the cardholder agreement.

Again, the pivotal question was what constitutes unauthorized use. Both the majority and dissenting opinions noted the TILA's definition of unauthorized use: "Use by a person other than the cardholder who does not have actual, implied, or apparent authority and from which the cardholder receives no benefit." While the majority and the dissent seem to agree that Mr. Jones was not a "cardholder" within the meaning of the TILA and that Mr. Jones had no actual or implied authority (nor did the bank contend there was such authority), the opinions split on whether he acted with "*apparent* authority."

The majority said that apparent authority exists when "a person has created such an appearance of things that it causes a third party reasonably and prudently to believe that a second party has the power to act on behalf of the first person." Mrs. Jones created such an appearance when she requested that her husband receive a credit card

22

bearing his own name and signature, leading third party merchants reasonably and prudently to conclude that Mr. Jones was authorized to use the card even if in fact he was not. Mrs. Jones' notification to the bank that further use of the credit card by Mr. Jones was unauthorized did not revoke his apparent authority. Therefore, the majority held that Mr. Jones acted with apparent authority and the TILA did not apply to limit Mrs. Jones' liability. The majority then turned to the terms of the cardholder agreement and found that because Mrs. Jones did not surrender all of the credit cards issued on her account immediately on the bank's request, she was liable for all the charges incurred.

This case stands for the proposition that use of a credit card by a separated spouse after cardholder notification that the use is no longer authorized is not "unauthorized use" within the meaning of the TILA because such use is clothed with *apparent* authority. Critics writing about this holding have suggested that what the courts should do and are likely to do is to follow the principles of the law of agency and determine in these situations whether the cardholder acted *reasonably* in each case. The best result in the case just described would have been to require the cardholder to notify the bank and return her own cards, and not impose the unreasonable burden of returning all of the credit cards issued on her account.

Many states have enacted legislation limiting liability of credit card holders. New York State enacted a statute limiting liability for use of lost or stolen cards. North Dakota and Vermont limit liability of the owner of a credit card for unauthorized use to $100 provided adequate notice of loss is given to the issuer of the card, the unauthorized use occurs prior to the notice, and the user of the card can be identified by signature or photograph. California, Kansas, Maine, Massachusetts,

New Mexico, and Wyoming have similar statutes except the amount is limited to $50. In Illinois maximum liability for card without signature panel $25; with, $50. While in Maryland, the holder is not liable for any unauthorized use.

A large number of states have enacted statutes which provide that a person who receives an unsolicited credit card which he does not accept by use or authorization of use is not responsible for any liability resulting from its loss or theft; failure to return or destroy an unsolicited card does not constitute acceptance. Included in these states are Alaska, California, Connecticut, Florida, Hawaii, Illinois, Kansas, Maryland, Massachusetts, Minnesota, New Mexico, New York, North Dakota, Ohio, Rhode Island, Tennessee, Vermont, Virginia, Wisconsin, and Wyoming. In Connecticut, Delaware, Florida, Hawaii, New York and Rhode Island, the unauthorized issuance of credit cards is in itself a crime; in Illinois, it is a business offense resulting in a maximum fine of $500. Delaware law requires that an issuer of an unsolicited credit card must send the recipient fourteen days notice before the card is mailed to him. The notice must be accompanied by a conspicuous statement that the recipient has a right of refusal. Additionally, a prepaid return envelope must be included. But use of the card will constitute acceptance.

A number of cases have held that if a credit cardholder allows another person to use his credit card and that person exceeds the authority given by charging to the account more than he was authorized to charge against it, the credit cardholder remains responsible for those excessive purchases. In *Martin v. American Express, Inc.* 361 So 2d 597, the cardholder authorized the other person not to exceed $500 and wrote to the credit card company requesting that amounts charged not exceed

$1,000. The cardholder could not rely on the statute and was liable for any purchases made through use of his card by anyone authorized to use it. Unauthorized use of a card occurs only where there is no actual, implied or apparent authority.

In one case a husband requested and received a bank credit card, and then some time later initiated proceedings so that his wife might receive a card, without her filling out or signing an application. The wife was issued a card under the husband's account. He received cash advances which were charged to his account but which he did not repay. The issuer could not hold the wife liable for the unpaid debts because she was held to be the recipient of a related card, and not an original cardholder. *Cleveland Trust Co. v. Snyder,* 380 NE 2d 354.

Chapter 3

CRIMINAL LIABILITY: STATE LEGISLATION

The general criminal statutes of most states make credit purchases made with a stolen credit card or otherwise illegally obtained cards the offense of *larceny*. Under most credit plans, the holder is required to sign a check, invoice or other document for the merchandise or services received. If someone other than the legitimate holder signs the holder's name to such a document without the holder's authority the crime of *forgery* is also committed.

A person who obtains a credit card by misrepresentation and then uses the card to purchase goods or services on credit commits larceny the same as one who directly obtains property from the owner by *false pretenses*. It may be possible to prosecute someone who obtains a credit card by false pretenses even though he does not use it. And by analogy to other forms of documents, the courts are likely to hold that the material alteration of a credit card such as by change of name, number of expiration date and subsequent use would constitute a criminal offense in the areas of forgery or larceny.

In a situation where a holder who uses his credit card after the expiration date or who is financially unable to pay for his credit purchases on a valid card there are unpredictable outcomes. While many states have enacted statutes making it a criminal offense to use a credit card after it has expired or revoked, it is questionable whether in the absence of such a statute a holder could be successfully prosecuted under general larceny statutes. This is especially unlikely if there is no strong showing of criminal intent to defraud.

Most states make it unlawful to use the credit card of another person for the purpose of obtaining credit without the consent of the person to whom the card was issued. *Knowing* use of an expired or revoked card to obtain goods or services on credit where notice of the revocation has been given to the person to whom the card was issued is also prohibited. But in some states the violation is restricted to knowing use with intent to defraud.

Where the statute provides that notice of revocation be given to the person to whom the card was issued, a provision is usually included that notice can be in person or by a writing sent by registered or certified mail in the United States mail addressed to such person at his last known address. The following states require notice of revocation in writing:

Alabama	Kansas	Pennsylvania
Arkansas	Kentucky	Rhode Island
Colorado	Louisiana	South Carolina
Florida	Maine	Tennessee
Georgia	Michigan	Texas
Hawaii	Mississippi	West Virginia
Idaho	Nevada	Wisconsin
Iowa	New Jersey	Wyoming
Indiana	Oklahoma	

In Alabama and Wyoming such notice can be either oral or written.

A few states provide that the presentation of an expired or revoked card is *prima facie* evidence of knowledge that the card is expired or revoked unless the purchaser within ten days after receipt of notice that the card has expired or been revoked at the time of the purchase, makes payment in full of the amount due on such purchase. The notice of revocation or expiration in that case must also state the amount due on such purchase.

28

Some states have included in their statutes relating to credit cards a prohibition against obtaining telephone, telegraph or other message service by fraudulent scheme, devise, means or method with intent to avoid payment of lawful charges for such services.

In most states misuse by a consumer of a credit card is a misdemeanor. California and Kansas make the violation a felony where the value of service, purchase, credit or benefit procured is $50 or more; in Hawaii, Kentucky, Michigan, Nevada, Tennessee, and Virginia it is $100 or more; in Delaware, Maryland, New Mexico, Nebraska, and Ohio it is $300 or more; in Arizona, Connecticut, New Hampshire, North Dakota, Pennsylvania, and Wisconsin it is $500 or more while in Colorado, Oregon, and Wyoming it is $2,000 or more.

California provides that one who, with intent to defraud, either forges, materially alters or counterfeits a credit card is guilty of a felony. Indiana makes felonies the procurement of property of any value through fraudulent misuse of credit cards. The Texas statute also makes a third offense a felony regardless of the amount involved. Utah provides that improper use of a credit card to obtain goods or services for a value of $2,500 is a felony of the second degree.

The usual penalty provided by the statutes when the amount involved is under $50 is a fine of not more than $100 or 30 days' imprisonment, or both; when the amount is more than $50, a fine of not less than $100, or imprisonment for not more than one year, or both. Where the violation of the act is a felony, the penalty is more severe. In Virginia, for example, confinement in a penitentiary can be for as long as three years where the amount involved is $100, or more.

As a review of the statutes in Appendix A will reveal, many states have enacted statutes regulating frauds and misuses. In Colorado it is a crime to purchase goods or services on credit under an assumed or fictitious name *with intent to cheat or defraud.* The statute applies to the fraudulent use of credit cards as well as other means of illegally obtaining goods and services. In Utah, provisions dealing with fraudulent use of credit cards include both forged and expired credit cards. In Virginia, the credit card law encompasses use of cards to obtain money, goods, or services that debit the account of the card holder with his bank even though no credit was actually extended.

The Illinois Credit Card Act regulates fraud and misuses in connection with the issuance of credit cards. The law details and sets out penalties for specified acts done with intent to make fraudulent use of a credit card. Among the violations regulated are the fraudulent use, sale, possession or transfer of any credit card without the knowledge or permission of the cardholder or issuer as well as the fraudulent use, sale, possession or transfer of forged, counterfeited, altered, revoked, or expired credit cards.

Nevada law provides that any person who has in his possession or under his control two or more credit cards issued in the name or names of another person or persons is presumed to have obtained and to possess such credit cards with the knowledge that they have been stolen and with the intent to circulate, use, sell or transfer them with intent to defraud. Kentucky has a similar statute. The penalty for conviction of such a crime is imprisonment for not less than one year nor more than six years.

Under Montana's criminal code it is a deceptive practice to obtain property, labor or services by the unauthorized use of a credit card of another person or by use of revoked, cancelled, forged, altered or expired credit card. Texas also has a similar statute.

North Carolina has a Financial Transaction Credit Card Theft Statute which subjects to criminal penalties anyone who takes, keeps, or uses a credit card without the proper owner's consent or who retains possession with intent to use a card that he knows to be lost, mislaid, or delivered to him by mistake. Possession of a card not in the name of the possessor, or in the name of a family member of the possessor, is a *prima facie* evidence of theft.

Model Penal Law

When the American Law Institute included Section 224.6 dealing with the fraudulent use of credit cards it spoke of what was "a relatively new credit device" in its Commentary. It was included to fill "a potential gap in the law relating to obtaining property by false pretenses." The commentators noted that it was questionable whether other sections of the Model Code which covered the theft of property or services by deception reached the credit card situation because the user of a stolen or cancelled credit card arguably does not obtain property or services by means of any deception practiced on the person providing the property or services. The actor's implicit representation that the issuer of the card will reimburse the merchant is true: the seller will collect from the issuer of the credit card because issuers assume the risk of misuse of cards in order to encourage sellers to honor the cards readily. It is, therefore, the non-deceived issuer who is the victim of the practice.

Most of the criminal codes drawn up among the states have included a separate offense dealing with the subject of credit card fraud. Newer sections covering theft or forgery of a credit card itself have been added in most recent years. Several states, have not dealt separately with stealing a credit card or theft with a credit card but have included offenses under general theft statutes.

Section 224.6 of the Model Code (see Appendix C) provides that it is an offense to use a credit card for the purpose of obtaining property or services with knowledge that the card is stolen, forged, revoked, cancelled, or for any other unauthorized reason. Some of the state codes have followed the Model Code in not requiring any criminal state of mind beyond knowledge that use of the card is unauthorized. On the other hand, a number of the newer codes particularly as well as many older statutes, require an "intent to defraud."

The definition of a credit card in the Code is a "writing or other evidence of an undertaking to pay for property or services delivered or rendered to or upon the order of a designated person or bearer." This would seem to apply only to the use of an actual card that evidences an obligation on the part of the issuer. The Commentary suggests that it would not appear to cover the situation where a person uses a fictitious number on a mail order form or gives a ficitious telephone credit card number to an operator. Many new codes have explicitly covered these situations in legislation against credit card fraud. For example, the Kansas statute defines unlawful use of a credit card to include "Using a falsified, mutilated, altered or nonexistent credit card or a number or description thereof."

Section 224.6 distinguishes between the use of stolen, forged, revoked, or cancelled cards, on the one hand, and use of cards outside the authorization of the issuer, on the other. The second sentence of the section gives the actor an affirmative defense in the latter case upon proof by a preponderance of the evidence that he had the purpose and ability to meet all obligations to the issuer arising out of his use of the card. The situations chiefly contemplated were those of the holder of an expired credit card and those where the user exceeded credit limits established by

32

the user. Cards are readily renewable and credit limits easily exceeded.

The rationale for this view is that it seems undesirable to penalize good-faith use of a card by someone to whom it had been issued merely because he has delayed or omitted some minor step required to perfect or maintain his right to continue to use the credit of the issuer or because he has failed adequately to keep track of all charges previous incurred. In any event, only a very few states have followed the Model Penal Code in providing an affirmative defense for good-faith use. Those states that include "intent to defraud" as an element of the offense rely on this *mens rea* requirement to cover these situations.

In *grading* credit card offenses, the Code grades such offenses as a felony of the third degree where the amount involved is over $500 and otherwise as a misdemeanor. This parallels the case of bad checks were the offense is not reduced to the level of a petty misdemeanor even when the amount involved is quite small. The rationale, in the case of both credit cards lend themselves to repeated violations by transients so as to undermine reliance on useful credit mechanisms.

As the earlier discussion of the state statutes reveals, the states have adopted a variety of approaches and standards in establishing misdemeanor and felony categories. A few states have followed the Model Code approach, although the dividing point between felony and misdemeanor varies.

A number of states agree in principle with using the amount involved as a means to distinguish between felony and misdemeanor, but define the amount involved not from a single transaction but from a series of transactions within a given time period.

Two states, Georgia and Texas, make the fraudulent use of a credit card an automatic felony. New Jersey grades all credit card fraud as a crime of the fourth degree, which carries a maximum term of 18 months. Utah has a four-tier scheme of grading which ranges from a class B misdemeanor for goods valued at less than $100 to a felony of the second degree for goods in excess of $2,500.

Chapter 4

CREDIT CARD ABUSE: FEDERAL LEGISLATION

In addition to the possibilities of prosecution under the state statutes referred to in the previous chapter, the misuse of a credit card under certain circumstances may give rise to a prosecution under various *federal* criminal statutes.

The federal mail fraud statute (18 USCS #1341) prohibits the use or causing the use of the mails "for the purpose of executing" a scheme or artifice to defraud. This statute has been interpreted by the federal courts to be broad enough to cover the procurement of a credit card by misrepresentation in order to perpetrate a fraud, or to carry out a fraud through the use of a stolen or forged credit card, providing that the use of the mails was a significant step in the execution of the fraudulent scheme. In *United States v. Maze,* 414 U.S. 395, 94 S. Ct. 645, it was held that this statute was not violated by a defendant's unlawful use of another person's bank credit card at out-of-state motels which resulted in mailing sales invoices by the motels to the bank and by the bank to the credit card owner. The Supreme Court's reasoning was that since the mailings were not sufficiently related to the defendant's scheme his conduct was not brought within the statute because his scheme reached "fruition" when he checked out of the motels. The mails had been used for the purpose of adjusting the accounts between the motels, bank, and card owner, rather than "for the purpose of executing" the defendant's scheme as required by the statute.

In *United States v. Stein,* 500 F 2d 678, a California case, the defendant's acts were construed as being in violation of the mail fraud statute where applications for credit cards containing fraudulent credit references and other fraudulent statements were mailed to the credit card issuer and the defendant used credit cards to charge $11,000 in goods and services.

A fraudulent scheme involving the use of stolen credit cards could be prosecuted under the mail fraud statute rather than Section 1644 of the Federal Truth in Lending Act (discussed below), which prohibits the fraudulent use of credit cards specifically, because the plan, which involved participation of merchants, did not reach fruition at the presentation of the cards, but only after the bank or the credit card company had mailed payment to the merchants in response to a mailing of invoices. The court said that this rendered the use of the mail as integral to the scheme. *United States v. Adamo,* 534 F 2d 31.

It is within the power of the court to require restitution of any amount up to the entire elicit gain from a scheme where a defendant is convicted under the mail fraud statute.

The Federal Truth in Lending Law

The Federal Truth in Lending Law also imposes criminal liability for the wrongful use of credit cards. Section 1644 of Title 15 (see Appendix B). In 1974 this section was rewritten for the purpose of liberalizing federal assistance to cope with the rapidly rising problem of credit card fraud. The statute, as amended, broadly proscribes fraudulent use of credit cards in interstate or foreign commerce, or transactions affecting such commerce. Counterfeit, fictitious, altered, forged, lost, stolen, or fraudulently obtained credit cards are dealt with by the statute in defining various offenses, the prescribed punishment for which is a fine of not more than $10,000 or imprisonment of not more than ten years, or both.

A common element in several of the offenses is the requirement that the money, goods, services, or other things of value involved must have an *aggregate* value of $1,000 or more within any one-year period. Other offenses, such as those involving unlawful intent, transporting, or attempting to transport such credit cards, or using any instrumentality of interstate or foreign commerce to sell or transport them, have no valuation requirement. Special provision is made with respect to tickets for interstate or foreign transportation.

United States v. De Biasi, 712 F. 2d 785, offers a good example how the courts construe the required *intent* to defraud. The defendant contended that the evidence did not show that he knew or should have known that each counterfeit credit card he produced had a credit limit in excess of $1,000 and that he specifically intended that each card be used to obtain more than $1,000 in a single transaction affecting interstate commerce. The court rejected this contention and affirmed the conviction, holding that the interstate commerce and the $1,000 monetary threshold elements of the statute are solely jurisdictional and need not be in the mind of a defendant who knowingly joins a conspiracy which envisioned the maximum use of each counterfeit credit card, where each counterfeit card could in fact be used to obtain over $1,000 in goods and services and would necessarily affect interstate commerce.

The defendant in this case had been involved in a conspiracy to commit bank and wire fraud through the use of counterfeit credit cards whereby he would receive blank credit card slips from a merchant and, for a fee, imprint the slips with a card number, cardholder name, and cardholder signature using counterfeit credit cards. The court reasoned that it is the *agreement* that particular cards whose credit limit exceeds $1,000 would ultimately be used in transactions affecting interstate commerce to obtain as much money as possible by the merchant

37

purchaser, standing alone, that gives rise to a sufficient threat to interstate transactions as to trigger federal jurisdiction, adding that the defendant's intent and knowledge with respect to the interstate commerce and $1,000 monetary requirements are simply irrelevant to whether federal jurisdiction exists.

One of the most highly ligitated elements in the statute is (d) in Section 1644. This deals with the construction of "fraudulently obtained."

In *United States v. Kaye,* 545 F. 2d 491, the defendant was convicted of using a fraudulently obtained credit card to obtain goods and services. On appeal, the court struck down the defendant's argument that the two credit cards in question were not "fraudulently obtained" because the companies would have issued cards in spite of false and misleading cases made by the defendant in his applications for such cards. The defendant in this case made false statement on his application for credit cards relating to his ownership interest in a business, his income, and his business address. While observing that representatives of the issuing companies testified that the cards would probably have been issued had the truth been known, the court upheld the jury's finding that the defendant misstated his intention to pay for the charges at the time he applied for the cards, noting that the issuing companies would not have issued the cards had they known of the defendant's intent not to pay his debts. In response to the defendant's challenge to the sufficiency of the evidence with respect to the jury's finding that the cards were fraudulently obtained, the court took the position that it could not say that it was unreasonable for the jury to conclude that the defendant intended not to pay the charges at the time he applied for the cards, and that this constituted fraudulent obtainment.

It has been held by the courts that criminal fraud requires only proof of "tendency to induce reliance," rather than showing actual reliance in order to establish that the credit card was fraudulently obtained within the meaning of this statute. In *United States v. Chapman,* 591 F. 2d 1287, the court upheld the conviction, stating that the phrase "fraudulently obtained" does not require proof of reliance by the innocent party upon false or misleading statement made by the defendant. Here the court struck down the defendant's contention that the lower court erred in denying admission of a "telephone credit report" which tended to prove that the bank was aware that his credit application contained false statements and that the bank issued the card despite his knowledge. The defendant in this case had made several false statements on his credit card application, statements which falsely enhanced his financial status. Following the receipt of his credit card, the defendant made charges but failed to make payments for the credit purchases. In response to the defendant's contention that proof of actual reliance is necessary to establish that a card was fraudulently obtained within the meaning of the statute, the court noted that criminal fraud required only proof of a "tendency to induce reliance," rather than a showing of actual reliance.

The court here stated that the defendant was essentially arguing that the statute incorporates the elements of civil fraud, including proof of actual reliance. However, the court took the position that it is reasonable to distinguish between civil and criminal fraud because in civil fraud, reliance is necessary to show actual injury, while criminal law goes further in seeking to deter and punish attempt, thereby making the success of the fraudulent scheme irrelevant.

It would be useful at this point to consider a case where the court held that the credit cards in issue were not "fraudulently obtained" within the meaning of the statute, and dismissed the indictment.

The stipulated facts were that the credit cards were obtained by the original card holders without the intent to defraud the issuing companies. The cards were sold or given to the defendants with the knowledge of the original card holders that the defendants would use the cards to make charges without paying for them. The original card holders reported the cards as lost or stolen. Taking the position that the cards were neither fraudulently obtained from the issuer by the original card holder nor fraudulently obtained from the card holders by the defendants since the cards were given or sold by the card holders and not stolen from them, the court refused to accept the government's argument that the cards were fraudulently obtained from the card issuers.

The court stated that the fallacy of the government's argument was that it confused or equated "fraudulently *obtained*" and obtaining with fraudulent *intent*, whereby the defendants procured the cards with the intent to use them to obtain goods or services without paying for them. In the court's view, fraudulently obtaining and fraudulent intent are two separate and distinct elements of this offense, taking the position that the requirement of a false act distinct from a fraudulent intent is implicit in the text of the statute. The opinion noted that courts which have examined the meaning of "fraudulently obtained" in Section 1644 have uniformly found some deceitful or false action by the *original holder* with regard *to the issuer,* and that in cases where the card was subsequently obtained by third parties from the original holder, some deception of or theft from the original card holder was necessary for conviction.

Perhaps one of the "trickiest" problems in the area of the law of fraudulent credit card use is the developing construction of what is a "credit card" in specific situations.

United States v. Bice-Bey, 701 F. 2d 1086, is a fairly recent case which points up the problem. The defendant was convicted of violating Section 1644(a) by making false credit card telephone orders. The court upheld the defendant's conviction, rejecting her argument that she could not be convicted under the statute because the government failed to show that she made any use whatsoever of a credit card, as opposed to a credit card number, or that she obtained the numbers by theft or fraud rather than in some lawful manner.

In rejecting the argument that Section 1644 is concerned with the misappropriation and misuse of the plastic card itself and not of the credit account number to which the card witnesses, the court reasoned that the defendants suggested reading of the statute was overliteralistic. The core element of a "credit card," the court stated, is the account number, not the piece of plastic. The court pointed out, as this case illustrated, that the "credit card" can be used over the telephone without the seller ever seeing the plastic card itself Noting that the credit numbers used by the defendant were not hers and she had no authorization to use them, the court reasoned that if she had obtained them by ascertaining secretly the numbers belonging to the actual card holders, she was in effect stealing or fraudulently obtaining the essential element of the cards. In conclusion, then, by representing credit card numbers belonging to other persons as credit accounts belonging to herself or a third party, the defendant was using a fictitious "credit device" within the meaning of Section 1602(k) defining "credit card" in the Truth in Lending Act. Given the widespread promotion

41

by issuers and merchants and use by card holders, this view of telephoned orders *via* credit cards is of great importance in the business world.

On the other hand, in *United States v. Calihan,* 666 F. 2d 422, a case in which the defendant was convicted on four counts of transporting in interstate commerce fraudulently obtained credit cards in violation of Section 1644(b), as well as one count of using an instrumentality of interstate commerce to transport fraudulently obtained credit cards in violation of Section 1644(c), the court overturned the defendant's conviction, stating that the defendant's conduct could not have fallen within the scope of the statute because Section 1644 refers only to credit cards themselves and not to account numbers, and the defendant in this case never actually held any of the cards.

The defendant in this case was alleged to have engaged in interstate communications by telephone whereby he fraudulently obtained credit card numbers. It was never alleged that the defendant transported the cards themselves. Expressing the view that it is logical to suppose that Congress intended to protect credit accounts by protecting the credit cards that are the principal instruments of their use, the court held that the term "credit card" as used in Section 1644 means the small, flat tablet upon which a credit account number is imprinted, but does not mean that number alone. Contrary to most other holdings, the court here stated that a narrow reading of the term "credit card" is indicated by the fact that the Congress has already provided for the fraudulent use of credit card account numbers in statutes prohibiting wire and mail fraud, and that to leave credit card account numbers out of Section 1644 would not leave their abuse unpunished.

The Fair Credit Billing Act

The Fair Credit Billing amendments passed in 1974 (15 U.S.C. Sections 1666a-1666j) imposing a number of substantive requirements on creditors, including not only mandatory correction of billing errors, but also the regulation of information given to credit reporting agencies, the prohibition against finance charges for statements mailed less than fourteen days before payment is due, the requirement that payments be credited promptly and that excess payments be either credited to the consumer's account or refunded.

The Fair Credit Billing amendments also forbid a card issuer from prohibiting a merchant who honors the card from offering a discount for cash payment — clearly a provision which has nothing to do with disclosure. A parallel provision prohibits a card issuer from requiring sellers to procure tie-in services and prohibits offsets against a cardholder's deposit account unless authorized in writing. Finally, the Fair Credit Billing provisions preserve a cardholder's claims and defenses other than tort claims) arising out of credit card transactions where the obligor has made a good faith attempt to obtain satisfactory resolution of the problem with the merchant, the amount of the initial transaction exceeds $50, and the place where the initial transaction occurred was in the same state as the mailing address of the cardholder or within one hundred miles from that address. However, where the card issuer and the merchant are the same or related person or where the card issuer has participated in the merchant's solicitation, the cardholder need only make a good faith attempt to obtain a satisfactory resolution of the disagreement in order to preserve claims and defenses.

Appendix A
STATE CREDIT CARD LAWS: SELECTED STATUTES

ALABAMA STATUTES ANNOTATED

§ 13A-9-14. Illegal possession of or fraudulent use of credit card or debit card.

(a) A person commits the crime of illegal possession of a credit or debit card if, knowing that he does not have the consent of the owner, he takes, exercises control over or otherwise uses such card.

(b) A person commits the crime of fraudulent use of a credit or debit card if he uses, attempts to use or allows to be used, a credit card or debit card for the purpose of obtaining property, services or anything else of value with knowledge that:

(1) The card is stolen; or

(2) The card has been revoked or cancelled; or

(3) For any other reason his use of the card is unauthorized by either the issuer or the person to whom the credit card or debit card is issued.

The mere use by the original issuee of a credit card or debit card which has expired is not within the provisions of subdivision (b)(3) of this section.

(c) "Credit card" means any instrument, writing or other evidence, whether known as a credit card, credit plate, charge or by any other name, which purports to evidence an undertaking to pay for property or services delivered or rendered to or upon the order of a designated person or bearer.

(d) "Debit card" means any instrument or writing or other evidence known by any name issued with or without fee by an issuer for the use of a depositor in obtaining money, goods, services or anything else of value, payment of which is made against funds previously deposited in an account with the issuer.

45

(e) Illegal possession of or fraudulent use of a credit card or debit card is a Class C felony.

§ 13A-9-15. Reporting of credit card lost, stolen or mislaid.

(a) Any person who reports or attempts to report a credit card as being lost, stolen or mislaid knowing the report to be false violates this subsection and shall be fined not more than $1,000.00 or imprisoned not more than one year, or both.

(b) Any cardholder who, with intent to defraud, uses a credit card which has previously been reported lost, stolen or mislaid violates this subsection and shall be fined not more than $1,000.00 or imprisoned not more than one year, or both.

ALASKA STATUTES

Sec. 06.05.208. Revolving credit plans.

(a) A bank may extend credit under an agreement with a buyer of goods or services under which one or more advances may be made from time to time by the bank for the account of the buyer by means of the bank purchasing from a seller of goods or services instruments evidencing obligations arising out of sales made by the seller to the buyer.

(b) A bank may, in the case of extensions of credit made under this section, charge, collect and receive a service charge not in excess of the limitations for the same service charges and transactions as provided in AS 45.10.120(c).

(c) The bank shall supply the buyer with whom an agreement is made under (a) of this section, a statement setting out the maximum service charge permitted under AS 45.10.120(c). (§ 2 ch 63 SLA 1969)

Sec. 06.05.209. Issue of credit cards.

(a) A bank is not prohibited from issuing unsolicited credit cards or other similar credit granting devices but the bank may not hold the customer liable for charges made on a credit card or other device before its acceptance by the customer. Before an unsolicited card is considered accepted by the customer, the customer shall execute and furnish to the bank a written statement of acceptance.

(b) A bank may issue a credit card or other similar credit-granting device to a customer for obtaining money, goods, services or anything else of value and the bank, when credit is extended under this section, may impose a service charge not in excess of the limits for service charges provided in AS 45.10.120(c). However, in addition, when cash is advanced under this section, the bank may impose a setup charge which does not exceed three per cent of the funds advanced, or $12, whichever is less, except that on loans of under $100 a minimum not exceeding $3 may be charged.

Sec. 11.46.285. Fraudulent use of a credit card.

(a) A person commits the crime of fraudulent use of a credit card if, with intent to defraud, the person uses a credit card to obtain property or services with knowledge that

(1) the card is stolen or forged;

(2) the card is expired or has been revoked or cancelled; or

(3) for any other reason that person's use of the card is unauthorized by either the issuer or the person to whom the credit card is issued.

(b) Fraudulent use of a credit card is

(1) a class C felony if the value of the property or services obtained is $500 or more;

(2) a class A misdemeanor if the value of the property or services obtained is $50 or more but less than $500;

(3) a class B misdemeanor if the value of the property or services obtained is less than $50.

Sec. 11.46.290. Obtaining a credit card by fraudulent means.

(a) A person commits the crime of obtaining a credit card by fraudulent means if

(1) the person buys a credit card from a person other than the issuer or, as other than the issuer, the person sells a credit card;

(2) with intent to defraud, the person obtains control of a credit card as a security for debt; or

47

(3) with intent to defraud, the person makes a false statement in an application for a credit card.

(b) Obtaining a credit card by fraudulent means under (a)(1) or (2) of this section is a class C felony. Obtaining a credit card by fraudulent means under (a)(3) of this section is a class A misdemeanor.

ARIZONA REVISED STATUTES

CREDIT CARD FRAUD

§ 13-2101. Definitions

In this chapter, unless the context otherwise requires:

1. "Cancelled or revoked credit card" means a credit card which is no longer valid because permission to use it has been suspended, revoked or terminated by the issuer of such credit card by written notice sent by certified or registered mail addressed to the person to whom such credit card was issued at such person's last known address. Proof that the written notice has been deposited as certified or registered matter in the United States mail addressed to the person to whom the credit card was issued at such person's last known address gives rise to an inference that the written notice has been given to the cardholder.

2. "Cardholder" means any person:

(a) Named on the face of a credit card to whom or for whose benefit the credit card is issued by an issuer; or

(b) In possession of a credit card with the consent of the person to whom the credit card was issued.

3. "Credit card" means any instrument or device, whether known as a credit card, credit plate, courtesy card or identification card or by any other name, issued with or without fee by issuer for the use of the cardholder in obtaining money, goods, services or anything else of value, either on credit or in possession or in consideration of an undertaking or guaranty by the issuer of the payment of a check drawn by the cardholder, upon a promise to pay in part or in full at a future time, whether or not all or any part of the indebtedness

represented by such promise to make deferred payment is secured or unsecured.

4. "Expired credit card" means a credit card which is no longer valid because the term shown on such credit card has elapsed.

5. "Incomplete credit card" means a credit card upon which part of the matter, other than the signature of the cardholder, which an insurer requires to appear before it can be used by a cardholder, has not been stamped, embossed, imprinted or written.

6. "Issuer" means any business organization or financial institution or its duly authorized agent, which issues a credit card.

7. "Merchant" means a person who is authorized by an issuer or a participating party to furnish money, goods, services or anything else of value upon presentation of that issuer's credit card by a cardholder.

8. "Participating party" means a business organization or financial institution which is obligated or permitted by contract to acquire from a merchant a sales slip or sales draft or instrument for the payment of money evidencing a credit card transaction and from whom an issuer is obligated or permitted by contract to acquire such sales slip, sales draft or instrument for the payment of money evidencing a credit and transaction.

9. "Receives or receiving" means acquiring possession or control of a credit card or accepting a credit card as security for a loan.

§ 13-2102. Theft of a credit card or obtaining a credit card by fraudulent means; classification

A. A person commits theft of a credit card or obtaining a credit card by fraudulent means if such person:

1. Takes a credit card from the possession, custody or control of any person without the cardholder's or issuer's consent through conduct defined in §§ 13—1802 and 13—1804; or

2. Receives a credit card knowing it to have been obtained illegally, lost, mislaid or delivered under a mistake as to the

identity or address of the cardholder and without lawful authority retains possession thereof with intent to use it, to sell it or to transfer it to a person other than the issuer or the cardholder; or

3. Sells, transfers or conveys a credit card with the intent to defraud; or

4. With intent to defraud, obtains possession, care, custody or control over a credit card as security for debt.

B. Theft of a credit card or obtaining a credit card by fraudulent means is a class 5 felony.

§ 13-21-3. Receipt of anything of value obtained by fraudulent use of a credit card; classification

A. A person, being a third party, commits receipt of anything of value obtained by fraudulent use of a credit card by buying or receiving money, goods, services or any other thing of value obtained in violation of § 13-2105, knowing or believing that it was so obtained.

B. Receipt of anything of value obtained by fraudulent use of a credit card is a class 1 misdemeanor if the value of the property bought is less than one hundred dollars. If the value of the property bought or received is one hundred dollars or more the offense is a class 6 felony. Amounts obtained by fraudulent use of a credit card pursuant to one scheme or course of conduct, whether from one or several persons, may be aggregated in determining the classification of offense.

§ 13-2104. Forgery of credit card; classification

A. A person commits forgery of a credit card if such person:

1. With intent to defraud, alters any credit card, falsely makes, manufactures, fabricates or causes to be made, manufactured or fabricated an instrument or device purporting to be a credit card without the express authorization of an issuer to do so, or falsely emboss or alters a credit card, or instrument or device purporting to be a credit card, or utters such a credit card or instrument or device purporting to be a credit card.

2. Other than the cardholder, with intent to defraud, signs

the name of any actual or fictitious person to a credit card or instrument for the payment of money which evidences a credit card transaction.

B. Forgery of a credit card is a class 6 felony.

§ 13-2105. Fraudulent use of a credit card; classification

A. A person commits fraudulent use of a credit card if such person:

1. With intent to defraud, uses, for the purposes of obtaining money, goods, services or any other thing of value, a credit card or credit card number obtained or retained in violation of this chapter or a credit card or credit card number which such person knows is forged, expired, cancelled or revoked; or

2. Obtains money, goods, services or any other thing of value by representing, without the consent of the cardholder, that he is the holder to a specified card or by representing that he is the holder of a credit card and such card has not in fact been issued.

B. Fraudulent use of a credit card is a class 1 misdemeanor. If the value of all money, goods, services and other things of value obtained in violation of this section exceeds one hundred dollars in any consecutive six-month period the offense is a class 6 felony.

ARKANSAS STATUTES ANNOTATED

41-2308 Fraudulent use of a credit card.—(1) A person commits the offense of fraudulent use of a credit card if, with purpose to defraud, he uses a credit card to obtain property or services with knowledge that:

(a) the card is stolen; or

(b) the card has been revoked or canceled; or

(c) the card is forged; or

(d) for any other reason his use of the card is unauthorized by either the issuer or the person to whom the credit card is issued.

(2) Fraudulent use of a credit card is a class C felony if the value of all money, goods, or services obtained during any six

(6) month period exceeds $100.00. Otherwise, it is a class A misdemeanor. [Acts 1975, No. 280, § 2308, p. 500.]

WEST'S ANNOTATED CALIFORNIA CODE (CIVIL)

§ 1747. Short title

This title may be cited as the "Song-Beverly Credit Card Act of 1971."

§ 1747.01. Legislative intent; conformance with federal law

It is the intent of the Legislature that the provisions of this title as to which there are similar provisions in the federal Truth in Lending Act, as amended (15 U.S.C. 1601, et seq.)[1], essentially conform, and be interpreted by anyone construing the provisions of this title to so conform, to the Truth in Lending Act and any rule, regulation, or interpretation promulgated thereunder by the Board of Governors of the Federal Reserve System, and any interpretation issued by an official or employee of the Federal Reserve System duly authorized to issue such interpretation.

§ 1747.02. Definitions

As used in this title:

(a) "Credit card" means any card, plate, coupon book, or other single credit device existing for the purpose of being used from time to time upon presentation to obtain money, property, labor, or services on credit. "Credit card" shall not mean any of the following:

(1) Any single credit device used to obtain telephone property, labor or services in any transaction under public utility tariffs.

(2) Any device that may be used to obtain credit pursuant to an electronic fund transfer but only if such credit is obtained under an agreement between a consumer and a financial institution to extend credit when the consumer's asset account is overdrawn or to maintain a specified minimum balance in the consumer's asset account.

(3) Any key or card key used at an automated dispensing outlet to obtain or purchase petroleum products, as defined in subdivision (c) of Section 13401 of the Business and Professions Code, which will be used primarily for business rather than personal or family purposes.

(b) "Accepted credit card" means any credit card which the cardholder has requested or applied for and received or has signed, or has used, or has authorized another person to use, for the purpose of obtaining money, property, labor, or services on credit. Any credit card issued in renewal of, or in substitution for, an accepted credit card becomes an accepted credit card when received by the cardholder, whether such card is issued by the same or a successor card issuer.

(c) "Card issuer" means any person who issues a credit card or the agent of such person for such purpose with respect to such card.

(d) "Cardholder" means a natural person to whom a credit card is issued for consumer credit purposes, or a natural person who has agreed with the card issuer to pay consumer credit obligations arising from the issuance of a credit card to another natural person. For purposes of Sections 1747.05, 1747.10 and 1747.20, the term includes any person to whom a credit card is issued for any purpose, including business, commercial, or agricultural use, or a person who has agreed with the card issuer to pay obligations arising from the issuance of such a credit card to another person.

(e) "Retailer" means every person other than a card issuer who furnishes money, goods, services, or anything else of value upon presentation of a credit card by a cardholder.

(f) "Unauthorized use" means the use of a credit card by a person, other than the cardholder, (i) who does not have actual, implied, or apparent authority for such use and (ii) from which the cardholder receives no benefit. "Unauthorized use" does not include the use of a credit card by a person who has been given authority by the cardholder to use the credit card. Any attempted termination by the cardholder of such person's authority is ineffective as against the card issuer until such time as the cardholder complies with such procedures as may be

53

required by the card issuer to terminate such authority. Notwithstanding the above, following the card issuer's receipt of oral or written notice from a cardholder indicating that it wishes to terminate the authority of a previously authorized user of a credit card, the card issuer shall follow its usual procedures for precluding any further use of a credit card by an unauthorized person.

(g) An "inquiry" is a writing which is posted by mail to the address of the card issuer to which payments are normally tendered, unless another address is specifically indicated on the statement for such purpose, then to such address, and which is received by the card issuer no later than 60 days after the card issuer transmitted the first periodic statement that reflects the alleged billing error, and which:

(1) Sets forth sufficient information to enable the card issuer to identify the cardholder and the account;

(2) Sufficiently identifies the billing error; and

(3) Sets forth information providing the basis for the cardholder's belief that such billing error exists.

(h) A "response" is a writing which is responsive to an inquiry and mailed to the cardholder's address last known to the card issuer.

(i) A "timely response" is a response which is mailed within two complete billing cycles, but in no event later than 90 days, after the card issuer receives an inquiry.

(j) A "billing error" means an error by omission or commission in (1) posting any debit or credit, or (2) in computation or similar error of an accounting nature contained in a statement given to the cardholder by the card issuer. A "billing error" does not mean any dispute with respect to value, quality or quantity of goods, services or other benefit obtained through use of a credit card.

(k) "Adequate notice" means a printed notice to a cardholder which sets forth the pertinent facts clearly and conspicuously so that a person against whom it is to operate could reasonably be expected to have noticed it and understood its meaning.

§ 1747.40. Failure of card issuer to give timely response to inquiry concerning debit or credit applicable to obligation

If a card issuer fails to give a timely response to an inquiry of a cardholder concerning any debit or credit applicable to an obligation incurred through the use of a credit card, he shall not be entitled to interest, finance charges, service charges, or any other charges thereon, from the date of mailing of the inquiry to the date of mailing of the response.

§ 1747.50. Correction of billing errors by card issuer; penalty for failure to correct; action

(a) Every card issuer shall correct any billing error made by the card issuer within two complete billing cycles, but in no event later than 90 days, after receiving an inquiry.

(b) Any card issuer who fails to correct a billing error made by the card issuer within the period prescribed by subdivision (a) shall not be entitled to the amount by which the outstanding balance of the cardholder's account is greater than the correct balance, not any interest, finance charges, service charges, or other charges on the obligation giving rise to the billing error.

(c) Any cardholder who is injured by a willful violation of this section may bring an action for the recovery of damages. Judgment may be entered for three times the amount at which actual damages are assessed. The cardholder shall be entitled to recover reasonable attorney's fees and costs incurred in the action.

§ 1747.80 Refusal to issue credit card for discriminatory reasons; penalty

(a) No card issuer shall refuse to issue a credit card to any person solely because of that person's race, religious creed, color, national origin, ancestry or sex.

(b) Any card issuer who willfully violates this section is liable for each and every such offense for the actual damages, and two hundred fifty dollars ($250) in addition thereto, suffered by any person denied a credit card solely for the reasons set forth in subdivision (a), and in addition such person may petition the court to order the card issuer to issue him a credit card upon such terms, conditions, and standards as the card issuer normally utilizes in granting credit to other individuals.

§ 1747.81. Married women; name on card

(a) If a card issuer has determined in the normal course of business that it will issue a card to a married woman, the card shall be issued bearing either the maiden name or married name of the woman, as the woman may direct.

(b) Card issuers may require that a married woman requesting a card in her maiden name open a new account in that name.

(C) The place where the initial transaction was in California, or, if not within California, then within 100 miles from the cardholder's current designated address in California.

(2) The limitations set forth in subparagraphs (B) and (C) of paragraph (1) with respect to a cardholder's right to assert claims and defenses against a card issuer shall not be applicable to any transaction in which the person honoring the credit card satisfies any of the following requirements:

(A) Is the same person as the card issuer.

(B) Is controlled by the card issuer.

(C) Is under direct or indirect common control with the card issuer.

(D) Is a franchised dealer in the card issuer's products or services.

(E) Has obtained the order for such transaction through a mail solicitation made by or participated in by the card issuer in which the cardholder is solicited to enter into such transaction by using the credit card issued by the card issuer.

(b) The amount of claims or defenses asserted by the cardholder may not exceed the amount of credit outstanding with respect to such transaction at the time the cardholder first notifies the card issuer or the person honoring the credit card of such claim or defense. For the purpose of determining the amount of credit outstanding, payments and credits to the cardholder's account are deemed to have been applied, in the order indicated, to the payment of the following:

(1) Late charges in the order of their entry to the account.

(2) Finance charges in order of their entry to the account.

(3) Debits to the account other than those set forth above, in the order in which each debit entry to the account was made.

(c) This section does not apply to the use of a check guarantee card or a debit card in connection with an overdraft credit plan, or to a check guarantee card used in connection with cash advance checks.

WEST'S ANNOTATED CALIFORNIA CODE (PENAL)

§ 484d. Definitions

As used in this section and Sections 484e to 484j, inclusive:

(1) "Cardholder" means any person to whom a credit card is issued or any person who has agreed with the card issuer to pay obligations arising from the issuance of a credit card to another person.

(2) "Credit card" means any card, plate, coupon book, or other credit device, *including, but not limited to, an account number or code or other means of account access which exists* for the purpose of being used from time to time upon presentation to obtain money, property, labor, or services on credit.

(3) "Expired credit card" means a credit card which shows on its face it has elapsed.

(4) "Card issuer" means any person who issues a credit card or the agent of such person with respect to such card.

(5) "Retailer" means every person who is authorized by an issuer to furnish money, goods, services or anything else of value upon presentation of a credit card by a cardholder.

(6) A credit card is "incomplete" if part of the matter other than the signature of the cardholder which an issuer requires to appear on the credit card before it can be used by a cardholder has not been stamped, embossed, imprinted, or written on it.

(7) "Revoked credit card" means a credit card which is no longer authorized for use by the issuer, such authorization

having been suspended or terminated and written notice thereof having been given to the cardholder.

§ 484e. Theft of credit card

(1) Every person who acquires a credit card from another without the cardholder's or issuer's consent or who, with knowledge that it has been so acquired, acquires the credit card, with intent to use it or to sell or transfer it to a person other than the issuer or the cardholder is guilty of petty theft.

(2) Every person who acquires a credit card that he knows to have been lost, mislaid, or delivered under a mistake as to the identity or address of the cardholder, and who retains possession with intent to use it or to sell it or to transfer it to a person other than the issuer or the cardholder is guilty of petty theft.

(3) Every person who sells, transfers, conveys, or receives a credit card with the intent to defraud is guilty of petty theft.

(4) Every person other than the issuer, who within any consecutive 12-month period, acquires credit cards issued in the names of four or more persons which he has reason to know were taken or retained under circumstances which constitute a violation of subdivisions (1), (2), or (3) of this section is guilty of grand theft.

§ 484f. Forgery of credit card

(1) Every person who, with intent to defraud, makes, alters, or embosses a card purporting to be a credit card or utters such a card is guilty of forgery.

(2) A person other than the cardholder or a person authorized by him who, with intent to defraud, signs the name of another or of a fictitious person to a credit card, sales slip, sales draft, or instrument for the payment of money which evidences a credit card transaction, is guilty of forgery.

§ 484g. Theft by use of credit card obtained or retained in violation of section 484e.

Every person, who with intent to defraud, (a) uses for the purpose of obtaining money, goods, services or anything else of value a credit card obtained or retained in violation of Section 484e or a credit card which he knows is forged, expired or revoked, or (b) obtains money, goods, services or anything else of value by representing without the consent of the cardholder that he is the holder of a credit card or by representing that he is the holder of a credit card and *the* card has not in fact been issued, is guilty of theft. If the value, of all money, goods, services and other things of value obtained in violation of this section exceeds *four* hundred dollars (*$400*) in any consecutive six-month period, then the same shall constitute grand theft.

CONNECTICUT GENERAL STATUTES ANNOTATED

§ 53a-128a. Credit card crimes. Definitions

As used in sections 53a-128a to 53a-128i, inclusive,

(a) "cardholder" or "holder of a card" means the person named on the face of a credit card to whom or for whose benefit the credit card is issued by an issuer;

(b) "credit card" means any instrument or device, whether known as a credit card, credit plate, or by any other name, issued with or without fee by an issuer for the user of the cardholder in obtaining money, goods, services or anything else of value on credit;

(c) "expired credit card" means a credit card which is no longer valid because the term shown on it has elapsed;

(d) "issuer" means the person which issues a credit card, or its agent duly authorized for that purpose;

(e) "participating party" means any person or any duly authorized agent of such person, which is obligated by contract to acquire from another person providing money, goods, services or anything else of value, a sales slip, sales draft or instrument for the payment of money, evidencing a credit card transaction, and from whom, directly or indirectly, the issuer is obligated by contract to acquire such sales slip, sales draft, instrument for the payment of money and the like;

(f) "receives" or "receiving" means acquiring possession, custody or control;

(g) "revoked credit card" means a credit card which is no

longer valid because permission to use it has been suspended or terminated by the issuer.

§ 53a-128b. False statements to procure issuance of credit card

Any person who make or causes to be made, either directly or indirectly, any false statement in writing, knowing it to be false and with intent that it be relied on, respecting his identity or that of any other person or his financial condition or that of any other person, for the purpose of procuring the issuance of a credit card, violates this section and is subject to the penalties set forth in subsection (a) of section 53a-128i.

(1971, P.A. 871, § 30.)

DELAWARE CODE ANNOTATED

§ 903. Unlawful use of credit card; class E felony; class A misdeamor.

(a) A person is guilty of unlawful use of a credit card when he uses or knowingly permits or encourages another to use a credit card for the purpose of obtaining property or services knowing that:

(1) The card is stolen, forged or fictitious; or

(2) The card belongs to another person who has not authorized its use; or

(3) The card has been revoked or canceled; or

(4) For any other reason his use of the card is unauthorized by the issuer.

(b) A person is guilty of unlawful use of a credit card where such person knowingly:

(1) Makes, possesses, sells, gives or otherwise transfers to another, or offers or advertises a credit card with the intent that it be used or with the knowledge or reason to believe that it will be used to obtain property or services without payment of the lawful charges therefor; or

(2) Publishes a credit card or code of an existing, canceled, revoked, expired or nonexistent credit card, or

the numbering or coding which is employed in the issuance of credit cards, with the intent that it be used or with knowledge or reason to believe that it will be used to avoid the payment of any property or services. As used in this section "publishes" means the communication of information to any 1 or more persons, either orally, in person or by telephone, radio or television, or in a writing of any kind, including without limitation a letter or memorandum, circular or handbill, newspaper or magazine article or book.

Unlawful use of a credit card is a class A misdemeanor, unless the value of the property or services secured or sought to be secured by means of the credit card exceeds $300, in which case it is a class E felony.

Amounts involved in unlawful use of a credit card pursuant to 1 scheme or course of conduct, whether from the same issuer or several issuers, may be aggregated in determining whether such unlawful use constitutes a class A misdemeanor or a class E felony under this section.

A person may be prosecuted and convicted under this section in such county or counties within Delaware where the property or services giving rise to the prosecution were solicited, or where the property or services were received or were attempted to be received or where the charges for the property or services were billable in the normal course of business.

§ 904. Definition of "credit card."

"Credit card" means a writing, number or other evidence of an undertaking to pay for property or services delivered or rendered to or upon order of a designated person or bearer.

§ 905. Intention and ability to meet obligations as affirmative defense.

In any prosecution for unauthorized use of a credit card under § 903(a)(4) of this title it is an affirmative defense that the accused had the intention and ability to meet all obligations to the issuer arising out of his use of the card.

§ 22-3822. Penalties for fraud.

(a) *Fraud in the 1st degree.*—(1) Any person convicted of fraud in the lst degree shall be fined not more than $5,000 or 3 times the value of the property obtained or lost, whichever is greater, or imprisoned for not more than 10 years, or both, if the value of the property obtained or lost is $250 or more; and

(2) Any person convicted of fraud in the lst degree shall be fined not more than $1,000 or imprisoned for not more than 1 year, or both, if the value of the property obtained or lost was less than $250.

(b) *Fraud in the 2nd degree.*—(1) Any person convicted of fraud in the 2nd degree shall be fined not more than $3,000 or 3 times the value of the property which was the object of the scheme or systematic course of conduct, whichever is greater, or imprisoned for not more than 3 years, or both, if the value of the property which was the object of the scheme or systematic course of conduct was $250 or more; and

(2) Any person convicted of fraud in the 2nd degree shall be fined out more than $1,000 or imprisoned for not more than 1 year, or both, if the value of the property which was the object of the scheme or systematic course of conduct was less than $250.

§ 22-3823. Credit card fraud.

(a) For the purpose of this section, the term "credit card" means an instrument or device, whether known as a credit card plate, debit card, or by any other name, issued by a person for use of the cardholder in obtaining property or services.

(b) A person commits the offense of credit card fraud if, with intent to defraud, that person obtains property of another by:

    (1) Knowingly using a credit card, or the number or description thereof, which has been issued to another person without the consent of the person to whom it was issued;

    (2) Knowingly using a credit card, or the number or description there which has been revoked or cancelled;

    (3) Knowingly using a falsified, mutilated, or altered

credit card number or description thereof; or

(4) Representing that he or she is the holder of a credit card and the credit card had not in fact been issued.

(c) A credit card is deemed cancelled or revoked when notice in writing thereof has been received by the named holder as shown on the credit card by the records of the issuer.

(d)(1) Any person convicted of credit card fraud shall be fined not more than $5,000 or imprisoned for not more than 10 years, or both, if the value of the property obtained is $250 or more.

(2) Any person convicted of credit card fraud shall be fined not more than $1,000 or imprisoned for not more than 1 year, or both, if the value of the property obtained is less than $250.

WEST'S FLORIDA STATUTES ANNOTATED

CREDIT CARD CRIMES

§ 817.58. Definitions

As used in ss. 817.57-817.685:

(1) "Cardholder" means the person or organization named on the face of a credit card to whom or for whose benefit the credit card is issued by an issuer.

(6) Forgery of credit card.—

(a) A person who, with intent to defraud a purported issuer or a person or organization providing money, goods, services, or anything else of value or any other person, falsely makes, falsely embosses, or falsely alters in any manner a credit card or utters such a credit card or who, with intent to defraud, has a counterfeit credit card or any invoice, voucher, sales draft, or other representation or manifestation of a counterfeit credit card in his possession, custody, or control is guilty of credit card forgery and is subject to the penalties set forth in s. 817.67(2).

(b) A person other than an authorized manufacturer or issuer who possesses two or more counterfeit credit cards is presumed to have violated this subsection.

(c) A person falsely makes a credit card when he makes or draws in whole or in part a device or instrument which purports to be the credit card of a named issuer but which is not such a credit card because the issuer did not authorize the making or drawing or when he alters a credit card which was validly issued.

(d) A person falsely embosses a credit card when, without the authorization of the named issuer, he completes a credit card by adding any of the matter, other than the signature of the cardholder, which an issuer requires to appear on the credit card before it can be used by a cardholder.

(7) Signing credit card of another.— A person other than the cardholder or a person authorized by him who, with intent to defraud the issuer or a person or organization providing money, goods, services, or anything else of value or any other person, signs a credit card violates this subsection and is subject to the penalties set forth in § 8.17.67(1).

817.61. Fraudulent use of credit cards

A person who, with intent to defraud the issuer or a person or organization providing money, goods, services, or anything else of value or any other person, uses, for the purpose of obtaining money, goods, services, or anything else of value, a credit card obtained or retained in violation of this part or a credit card which he knows is forged, or who obtains money, goods, services, or anything else of value by representing, without the consent of the cardholder, that he is the holder of a specified card or by representing that he is the holder of a card and such card has not in fact been issued violates this subsection. A person who, in any 6-month period, uses a credit card in violation of this section two or fewer times, or obtains money, goods, services, or anything else in violation of this section the value of which is less than $100, is subject to the penalties set forth in s. 817.67(1). A person who, in any 6-month period, uses a credit card in violation of this section more than two times, or obtains money, goods, services, or anything else in violation of this section the value of which is $100 or more, is subject to the penalties set forth in s. 817.67(2).

817.611. Traffic in counterfeit credit cards

Any person who traffics in or attempts to traffic in 10 or more counterfeit credit cards, invoices, vouchers, sales drafts, or other representations or manifestations of counterfeit credit cards, or credit card account numbers of another in any 6-month period is guilty of a felony of the second degree, punishable as provided in s. 775.082, s. 775.083, or s. 775.084.

817.612. Expired or revoked credit cards

A person who, with intent to defraud the issuer or a person or organization providing money, goods, services, or anything else of value, uses, for the purpose of obtaining money, goods, services, or anything else of value, a credit card which he knows is expired or revoked violates this section and is subject to the penalties set forth in s. 817.67(1). Knowledge of revocation shall be presumed to have been received by a cardholder 7 days after such notice has been mailed to him by first-class mail at the last-known address.

817.62. Fraud by person authorized to provide goods or services

(1) Illegally obtained or illegally possessed credit card; forged, revoked, or expired credit card.—A person who is authorized by an issuer to furnish money, goods, services, or anything else of value upon presentation of a credit card by the cardholder, or any agent or employee of such person, who, with intent to defraud the issuer or the cardholder, furnishes money, goods, services, or anything else of value upon presentation of a credit card obtained or retained in violation of this part or a credit card which he knows is forged, expired, or revoked violates this subsection and is subject to the penalties set forth in s. 817.67(1), if the value of all money, goods, services, and other things of value furnished in violation of this subsection does not exceed $100 in any 6-month period. The violator is subject to the penalties set forth in s. 817.67(2) if such value does exceed $100 in any 6-month period.

(2) Misrepresentation to issuer.—A person who is authorized by an issuer to furnish money, goods, services, or anything else of value upon presentation of a credit card by the cardholder, or any agent or employee of such person, who, with intent to defraud the issuer or the cardholder, fails to furnish money, goods, services, or anything else of value which he represents in writing to the issuer that he has furnished violates this subsection and is subject to the penalties set forth in s. 817.67(2).

OFFICIAL CODE OF GEORGIA ANNOTATED

ARTICLE 3
ILLEGAL USE OF FINANCIAL TRANSACTION CARDS

16-9-30. Definitions.

As used in this article, the term:

(1) "Automated banking device" means any machine which when properly activated by a financial transaction card and personal identification code may be used for any of the purposes for which a financial transaction card may be used.

(2) "Cardholder" means the person or organization named on the face of a financial transaction card to whom or for whose benefit the financial transaction card is issued by an issuer.

(3) "Expired financial transaction card" means a financial transaction card which is no longer valid because the term for which it was issued has elapsed.

(4) "Financial transaction card" or "FTC" means any instrument or device, whether known as a credit card, credit plate, bank services card, banking card, check guarantee card, debit card, or by any other name, issued with or without fee by an issuer for the use of the cardholder:

(A) In obtaining money, goods, services, or anything else of value;

(B) In certifying or guaranteeing to a person or business the availability to the cardholder of funds on deposit that are equal to or greater than the amount necessary to honor a draft or check payable to the order of such person or business; or

(C) In providing the cardholder access to a demand deposit account, savings account, or time deposit account for the purpose of:

(i) Making deposits of money or checks therein;

(ii) Withdrawing funds in the form of money, money orders, or traveler's checks therefrom;

(iii) Transferring funds from any demand deposit account, savings account, or time deposit account to any other demand deposit account, savings account, or time deposit account;

(iv) Transferring funds from any demand deposit account, savings account, or time deposit account to any credit card accounts, overdraft privilege accounts, loan accounts, or any other credit accounts in full or partial satisfaction of any outstanding balance owed existing therein;

(v) For the purchase of goods, services, or anything else of value; or

(vi) Obtaining information pertaining to any demand deposit account, savings account, or time deposit account.

(5) "Issuer" means the business organization or financial institution or its duly authorized agent which issues a financial transaction card.

(6) "Personal identification code" means a numeric or alphabetical code, signature, photograph, fingerprint, or any other means of electronic or mechanical confirmation used by the cardholder of a financial transaction card to permit authorized electronic use of that financial transaction card.

(7) "Presenting" means those actions taken by a cardholder or any person to introduce a financial transaction card into an automated banking device with or without utilization of a personal identification code or merely displaying or showing, with intent to defraud, a financial transaction card to the issuer or to any person or organization providing money, goods, services, or anything else of value or to any other entity.

(8) "Receives" or "receiving" means acquiring possession of or control of or accepting a financial transaction card as security for a loan.

(9) "Revoked financial transaction card" means a financial transaction card which is no longer valid because permission to use it has been suspended or terminated by the issuer.

16-9-31. Financial transaction card theft.

(a) A person commits the offense of financial transaction card theft when:

(1) He takes, obtains, or withholds a financial transaction card from the person, possession, custody, or control of another without the cardholder's consent; or who, with knowledge that it has been so taken, obtained, or withheld, receives the financial transaction card with intent to use it or to sell it or to transfer it to a person other than the issuer or the cardholder;

(2) He receives a financial transaction card that he knows to have been lost, mislaid, or delivered under a mistake as to the identity or address of the cardholder and he retains possession with intent to use it or sell it or to transfer it to a person other than the issuer or the cardholder;

(3) He, not being the issuer, sells a financial transaction card or buys a financial transaction card from a person other than the issuer; or

(4) He, not being the issuer, during any 12 month period receives two or more financial transaction cards in the names of persons which he has reason to know were taken or retained under circumstances which constitute a violation of paragraph (3) of subsection (a) of Code Section 16-9-33 and paragraph (3) of subsection (a) of this Code section.

16-9-32. Forgery and fraudulent practices

(b) Taking, obtaining, or withholding a financial transaction card without consent of the cardholder or issuer is included in conduct defined in Code Section 16-8-2 as the offense of theft by taking.

(c) Conviction of the offense of financial transaction card

theft is punishable as provided in subsection (b) of Code Section 16-9-38.

(d) When a person has in his possession or under his control two or more financial transaction cards issued in the names of persons other than members of his immediate family or without the consent of the cardholder, such possession shall be prima-facie evidence that the financial transaction cards have been obtained in violation of subsection (a) of this Code section.

16-9-33. Financial transaction card fraud.

(a) A person commits the offense of financial transaction card fraud when with intent to defraud the issuer; a person or organization providing money, goods, services, or anything else of value; or any other person, he:

(1) Uses for the purpose of obtaining money, goods, services, or anything else of value a financial transaction card obtained or retained or which was received with knowledge that it was obtained or retained in violation of Code Section 16-9-31 or 16-9-32, or a financial transaction card which he knows is forged, altered, expired, revoked, or was obtained as a result of a fraudulent application in violation of subsection (d) of this Code section;

(2) Obtains money, goods, services, or anything else of value by:

(A) Representing without the consent of the cardholder that he is the holder of a specified card;

(B) Presenting the financial transaction card without the authorization or permission of the cardholder; or

(C) Falsely representing that he is the holder of a card and such card has not in fact been issued;

(3) Obtains control over a financial transaction card as security for debt;

(4) Deposits into his account or any account by means of an automated banking device a false, fictitious, forged, altered, or counterfeit check, draft, money order, or any

other such document not his lawful or legal property; or

(5) Receives money, goods, services, or anything else of value as a result of a false, fictitious, forged, altered, or counterfeit check, draft, money order, or any other such document having been deposited into an account via an automated banking device, knowing at the time of receipt of the money, goods, services, or item of value that the document so deposited was false, fictitious, forged, altered, or counterfeit or that the above-deposited item was not his lawful or legal property.

(b) A person who is authorized by an issuer to furnish money, goods, services, or anything else of value upon presentation of a financial transaction card by the cardholder or any agent or employee of such person commits the offense of financial transaction card fraud when, with intent to defraud the issuer or the cardholder, he:

(1) Furnishes money, goods, services, or anything else of value upon presentation of a financial transaction card obtained or retained in violation of Code Section 16-9-31 or a financial transaction card which he knows is forged, expired, or revoked;

(2) Alters a charge ticket or purchase ticket to reflect a larger amount than that approved by the cardholder; or

(3) Fails to furnish money, goods, services, or anything else of value which he represents in writing to the issuer that he has furnished.

(c) Conviction of the offense of financial transaction card fraud as provided in subsection (a) or (b) of this Code section is punishable as provided in subsection (a) of Code Section 16-9-38 if the value of all money, goods, services, and other things of value furnished in violation of this Code section or if the difference between the value actually furnished and the value represented to the issuer to have been furnished in violation of this Code section does not exceed $100.00 in any six-month period. Conviction of the offense of financial transaction card fraud as provided in subsection (a) or (b) of this Code section is punishable as provided in subsection (b) of Code Section 16-9-38 if such value exceeds $100.00 in any six-month period.

(d) A person commits the offense of financial transaction card fraud when, upon application for a financial transaction card to an issuer, he knowingly makes or causes to be made a false statement or report relative to his name, occupation, employer, financial condition, assets, or liabilities or willfully and substantially overvalues any assets or willfully omits or substantially undervalues any indebtedness for the purposes of influencing the issuer to issue a financial transaction card. Fraud as provided in this subsection is punishable as provided in subsection (b) of Code Section 16-9-38.

(e) A cardholder commits the offense of financial transaction card fraud when he willfully, knowingly, and with an intent to defraud the issuer; a person or organization providing money, goods, services, or anything else of value; or any other person submits verbally or in writing to the issuer or any other person any false notice or report of the theft, loss, disappearance, or nonreceipt of his financial transaction card and personal identification code. Conviction of the offense of financial transaction card fraud as provided in this subsection is punishable as provided in subsection (b) of Code Section 16-9-38.

(f) In any prosecution for violation of this Code section, the state is not required to establish and it is no defense that some of the acts constituting the crime did not occur in this state or within one city, county, or local jurisdiction.

(g) For purposes of this Code section, revocation shall be construed to include either notice given in person or notice given in writing to the person to whom the financial transaction card and personal identification code was issued. Notice of revocation shall be immediate when notice is given in person. The sending of a notice in writing by registered or certified mail in the United States mail, duly stamped and addressed to such person at his last address known to the issuer, shall be prima-facie evidence that such notice was duly received after seven days from the date of deposit in the mail. If the address is located outside the United States, Puerto Rico, the Virgin Islands, the Canal Zone, and Canada, notice shall be presumed to have been received ten days after mailing by registered or certified mail.

71

§ 851-5 Fraud by person authorized to provide goods or services; penalties.

(b) A person who is authorized by an issuer to furnish money, goods, services, or anything else of value upon presentation of a credit card by the cardholder, or any agent or employee of such person, who, with intent to defraud the issuer or the cardholder, fails to furnish money, goods, services, or anything else of value which he represents in writing to the issuer that he has furnished violated this subsection and is subject to the penalties set forth in subsection 851-10(a), if the difference between the value of all money, goods, services, and anything else of value actually furnished and the value represented to the issuer to have been furnished does not exceed $100 in any six-month period; and is subject to the penalties set forth in subsection 851-10(b), if such difference exceeds $100 in any six-month period.

IDAHO CODE

28-41-301. General definitions.

(14) "Credit card" means a card or device issued under an arrangement pursuant to which a card issuer gives to a cardholder the privilege of obtaining credit from the card issuer or other person in purchasing or leasing property or services, obtaining loans, or otherwise. A transaction is "pursuant to a credit card" only if credit is obtained according to the terms of the arrangement by transmitting information contained on the card or device orally, in writing, by mechanical or electronic methods, or in any other manner. A transaction is not "pursuant to a credit card" if the card or device is used solely in that transaction to:

    (a) Identify the cardholder or evidence his credit-worthiness and credit is not obtained according to the terms of the arrangement;

    (b) Obtain a guarantee of payment from the cardholder's deposit account, whether or not the payment results in a credit extension to the cardholder by the card issuer; or

(c) Effect an immediate transfer of funds from the cardholder's deposit account by electronic or other means, whether or not the transfer results in a credit extension to the cardholder by the card issuer.

18-3123. Forgery of a financial transaction.

Any person who, with intent to defraud, counterfeits, falsely makes, embosses, or encodes magnetically or electronically any FTC, or who with intent to defraud, signs the name of another, or a ficticious [fictitious] name to an FTC, sales slip, sales draft or any instrument for the payment of money which evidences an FTC transaction, shall be guilty of forgery and shall be punished under the current forgery statutes of the state of Idaho.

18-3124. Fraudulent use of a financial transaction card.

It is a violation of the provisions of this section for any person with the intent to defraud:

(1) To knowingly obtain or attempt to obtain credit or to purchase or attempt to purchase any goods, property, or service, by the use of any false, ficticious [fictitious], counterfeit, revoked, expired or fraudulently obtained FTC, by any FTC credit number, or by the use of any FTC issued;

(2) To use an FTC to knowingly and willfully exceed the actual balance of the demand deposit account or time deposit account;

(3) To use an FTC to willfully exceed an authorized credit line in the amount of one thousand dollars ($1,000) or more, or fifty per cent (50%) of such authorized credit line, whichever is greater;

(4) To willfully deposit into his account or any other account by means of an automatic banking device, any false, forged, ficticious [fictitious], altered or counterfeit check draft, money order, or any other such document;

(5) To make application for an FTC to an issuer, while knowingly making or causing to be made a false statement or report relative to his name, occupation, financial condition,

assets, or to willfully and substantially under value any indebtedness for the purposes of influencing the issuer to issue an FTC.

SMITH-HURD ILLINOIS ANNOTATED STATUTES

Illinois Credit Card Act

6001. Definitions

§ 1. As used in this Act: (a) "Credit card" has the meaning set forth in Section 2.03 of the Illinois Credit Card Act, as now or hereafter amended; (b) "merchant credit card agreement" means a written agreement between a seller of goods, services or both, and the issuer of a credit card to any other party, pursuant to which the seller is obligated to accept credit cards; and (c) "credit card transaction" means a purchase and sale of goods, services or both, in which a seller, pursuant to a merchant credit card agreement, is obligated to accept a credit card and does accept the credit card in connection with such purchase and sale.

6002. Denial of credit card on account of unlawful discrimination prohibited

§ 1a. No person may be denied a credit card, upon proper application therefor, solely on account of unlawful discrimination, as defined and prohibited in Section 4-103 of the Illinois Human Rights Act. No question requesting any information concerning an applicant's marital status shall appear on any credit card application except in connection with an application for a joint account.

6003. Credit card applications—Contents

§ 1b. All credit card applications shall contain the following words verbatim:

a. No applicant may be denied a credit card on account of race, color, religion, national origin, ancestry, age (between 40 and 70), sex, marital status, physical or mental handicap

74

unrelated to the ability to pay or unfavorable discharge from military service.

b The applicant may request the reason for rejection of his or her application for a credit card.

c. No person need reapply for a credit card solely because of a change in marital status unless the change in marital status has caused a deterioration in the person's financial position.

d. A person may hold a credit card in any name permitted by law that he or she regularly uses and is generally known by, so long as no fraud is intended thereby.

6004. Applications conforming to federal law in compliance with Act

§ 1c. Notwithstanding the provisions of Sections 1a and 1b, credit card applications which conform to the requirements of the Federal Equal Credit Opportunity Act, amendments thereto, and any regulations issued or which may be issued thereunder shall be deemed to be in compliance with this Act.

6005. Liability to issuer of credit card or party to merchant credit card agreement

§ 2. Except to the extent provided in a merchant credit card agreement, a seller shall not be liable to the issuer of a credit card, or to any other party to a merchant credit card agreement or that party's agent or representative, for loss or damage to the issuer or other party resulting from a failure of the holder or user of the credit card to pay any obligation arising from a credit card transaction, provided that the seller has fully performed its obligation under the merchant credit card agreement and has not breached any of its obligations to the purchaser in the credit card transaction.

6006. Reasons for rejection of credit card application

§ 3. In every case where an applicant for a credit card is rejected by a credit card issuer, the applicant, upon request, shall be informed of the reasons for such rejection. Failure to comply with this section is a civil rights violation under Section 4—103 of the Illinois Human Rights Act.

6007. Financial status—Consideration upon application

§ 4. A credit card issuer shall, when requested, consider the financial status of a married couple when making a determination as to whether to issue a credit card.

A credit card issuer shall, upon request by an applicant, consider such person's financial status when making a determination as to whether to issue such person a credit card as an individual.

6008. Change in marital status—Notification of name change

§ 5. No credit card issuer shall require a person to reapply for credit solely because of a change in marital status. Nothing in this section shall prevent a credit card issuer from requiring notification of any name change.

KANSAS STATUTES ANNOTATED

ARTICLE 8
TRUTH IN LENDING

16-842. Liability of credit cardholder for unauthorized use, when; actions for enforcement of liability.

(a) A cardholder shall be liable for the unauthorized use of a credit card only if the card is an accepted credit card, the liability is not in excess of $50, the card issuer gives adequate notice to the cardholder of the potential liability and the unauthorized use occurs before the cardholder has notified the card issuer that an unauthorized use of the credit card has occurred or may occur as the result of loss, theft or otherwise. The card issuer shall provide a telephone number to be called by the cardholder in the event of loss or theft of the credit card. Notwithstanding the foregoing, no cardholder shall be liable for the unauthorized use of any credit card which was issued on or after the effective date of this section, and, after the expiration of 12 months following such effective date, no cardholder shall be liable for the unauthorized use of any credit card regardless of the date of its issuance, unless: (1) The conditions of liability specified in the preceding sentence are met; and (2) the card issuer has provided a method whereby the user of such card can be identified as the person authorized to use it. For the purposes of this section, a cardholder notifies a card issuer by taking such steps as may be reasonably required in the ordinary course of business to provide the card issuer with the pertinent information whether or not any particular officer, employee or agent of the card issuer does in fact receive such information.

(b) In any action by a card issuer to enforce liability for the use of a credit card, the burden of proof is upon the card issuer to show that the use was authorized or, if the use was unauthorized, then the burden of proof is upon the card issuer to show that the conditions of liability for the unauthorized use of a credit card, as set forth in subsection (a), have been met.

(c) Nothing in this section imposes liability upon a cardholder for the unauthorized use of a credit card in excess of the cardholder's liability for such use under other applicable law or under any agreement with the card issuer.

(d) Except as provided in this section, a cardholder incurs no liability from the unauthorized use of a credit card.

LOUISIANA REVISED STATUTES

§ 67.3. Unauthorized use of "Access Card" as theft; definitions

A. (1) "Access Card" shall mean and include any card, plate, paper, book or any other device issued to a person which authorizes such person to obtain credit, money, goods, services or anything of value, whether contemporaneous or not, by use of any credit or deferred payment plan with issuer or by use of debiting or charging such person's demand deposit or savings or time account with issuer or by debiting or charging any other funds such person has on deposit with issuer.

(2) "Revoked Access Card" as used herein shall mean an Access Card which has been cancelled or terminated by the issuer of said Access Card.

(3) "Person" as used herein shall mean and include natural persons, or any organization, or other entity.

(4) "Issuer" as used herein shall be the depository and/or creditor issuing the Access Card, directly or through another entity.

(5) The aggregate amount or value of credit, money, goods, services or anything else of value obtained shall determine the value of the misappropriation or taking in determining the penalty under R.S. 14:67 when the offender has obtained the credit, money, goods, services or anything else of value from any one issuer or the offender has used an Access Card, or referred to a nonexistent Access Card on two or more occasions within any consecutive ninety day period.

B. Whoever, directly or indirectly, by agent or otherwise, with intent to defraud, (1) uses a forged Access Card, (2) makes reference by number or other description to a nonexistent Access Card, (3) steals or wrongfully appropriates an Access Card, or (4) uses an Access Card belonging to another person without authority of said person; thereby obtaining, whether contemporaneously or not, credit, money, goods, services or anything of value shall be guilty of theft and shall be subject to the penalties provided for the crime of theft in R.S. 14:67.

C. Whoever, directly or indirectly, by agent or otherwise, with intent to defraud, uses a revoked Access Card, thereby obtaining, whether contemporaneously or not, credit, money, goods, services or anything of value shall be guilty of theft and shall be subject to the penalties provided for the crime of theft in R.S. 14:67. For purposes of this Subsection, it shall be presumptive evidence that a person used a revoked Access Card with intent to defraud if the said person, directly or indirectly, by agent or otherwise, uses the said Access Card after actually receiving oral or written notice that the Access Card has been cancelled or terminated, or if said person, directly or indirectly, by agent or otherwise, uses the said Access Card at a time period more than five days after written notice of the termination or cancellation of said Access Card has been deposited by registered or certified mail in the United States mail system. Said notice shall be addressed to the person to whom such Access Card has been issued at the last known address for such person as shown on the records of the issuer.

D. Whoever, directly or indirectly, by agent or otherwise, with the intent to defraud, uses an Access Card to obtain, whether contemporaneously or not, money, goods, services or anything of value, and the final payment for said items is to be made by debiting or charging said person's demand deposit or savings or time account with issuer, or by debiting or charging any other funds said person has on deposit with issuer, and there are not sufficient funds on deposit to the credit of said person with the issuer to make payment in full of said items obtained, said person shall have committed the crime of theft in R.S. 14:67. Said person's failure to pay the amount due on said items obtained:

(1) Within ten days after written notice of said amount due has been deposited by certified or registered mail in the United States mail system addressed to the person to whom such Access Card has been issued at the last known address for such person as shown on the records of issuer; or

(2) Within ten days of delivery or personal tender of said written notice shall be presumptive evidence of said person's intent to defraud.

E. As used herein and in R.S. 14:67, the Access Card itself shall be a thing of value, with a value less than one hundred dollars.

F. In addition to any other fine or penalty imposed under this Section or under R.S. 14:67, the court may, at its discretion, order as a part of the sentence, restitution.

MAINE REVISED STATUTES

CREDIT CARD RESTRICTIONS

§ 8—301. Issuance of credit cards

No credit card may be issued except in response to a request or application therefor. This prohibition does not apply to the issuance of a credit card in renewal of, or in substitution for, an accepted credit card.

1981, c. 243, § 25.

§8—302. Liability of holder of credit card

1. Except as provided in this section, a cardholder incurs no liability from the unauthorized use of a credit card. A cardholder shall be liable for the unauthorized use of a credit card only if:

A. The card is an accepted credit card;

B. The liability is not in excess of $50;

C. The card issuer gives adequate notice to the cardholder of the potential liability;

D. The card issuer has provided the cardholder with a description of a means by which the card issuer may be notified of loss or theft of the card, which description may be provided on the face or reverse side of the statement required by section 8-205, subsection 2, or on a separate notice accompanying the statement;

E. The unauthorized use occurs before the card issuer has been notified that an unauthorized use of the credit card has occurred or may occur as the result of loss, theft or otherwise; and

F. The card issuer has provided a method whereby the user of the card can be identified as the person authorized to use it.

2. For purposes of this section, a card issuer has been notified when such steps as may be reasonably required in the ordinary course of business to provide the card issuer with the pertinent information have been taken, whether or not any particular officer, employee or agent of the card issuer does in fact receive such information.

8-303. Credit card restrictions

1. With respect to a credit card which may be used for extensions of credit in sales transactions in which the seller is a person other than the card issuer, the card issuer may not, by contract or otherwise, prohibit any such seller from offering a

discount to a cardholder to induce the cardholder to pay by cash, check or similar means rather than use a credit card.

2. No seller in any sales transaction may impose a surcharge on a cardholder who elects to use a credit card in lieu of payment by cash, check or similar means.

3. With respect to any sales transaction, any discount offered by the seller for the purpose of inducing payment by cash, check or other means not involving the use of a credit card does not constitute a finance charge as determined under section 8-105, if that discount is offered to all prospective buyers and its availability is disclosed to all prospective buyers clearly and conspicuously.

4. Notwithstanding any agreement to the contrary, a card issuer may not require a seller, as a condition to participating in a credit card plan, to open an account with or procure any other service from the card issuer or its subsidiary or agent.

5. A card issuer may not take any action to offset a cardholder's indebtedness arising in connection with a consumer credit transaction under the relevant credit card plan against funds of the cardholder held on deposit with the card issuer unless:

A. This action was previously authorized in writing by the cardholder in accordance with a credit plan whereby the cardholder agrees periodically to pay debts incurred in his open-end credit account by permitting the card issuer periodically to deduct all or a portion of such debt from the cardholder's deposit account; and

B. This action with respect to any outstanding disputed amount not be taken by the card issuer upon request of the cardholder.

6. Rights of credit card customers are as follows.

A. Subject to the limitation contained in paragraph B, a card issuer who has issued a credit card to a cardholder pursuant to an open-end consumer credit plan is subject to all claims, other than tort claims, and defenses arising out of any transaction in which the credit card is used as a method of payment or extension of credit if:

(i) The obligor has made a good faith attempt to obtain satisfactory resolution of a disagreement or problem relative to the transaction from the person honoring the credit card;

(ii) The amount of the initial transaction exceeds $50; and

(iii) The place where the initial transaction occurred was in the same state as the mailing address previously provided by the cardholder or was within 100 miles from such address.

B. The limitations set forth in paragraph A, subparagraphs (ii) and (iii), with respect to an obligor's right to assert claims and defenses against a card issuer are not applicable to any transaction in which the person honoring the credit card:

(i) Is the same person as the card issuer;

(ii) Is controlled by the card issuer;

(iii) Is under direct or indirect common control with the card issuer;

(iv) Is a franchised dealer in the card issuer's products or services; or

(v) Has obtained the order for such transaction through a mail solicitation made by or participated in by the card issuer in which the cardholder is solicited to enter into the transaction by using the credit card issued by the card issuer.

C. The amount of claims or defenses asserted by the cardholder may not exceed the amount of credit outstanding with respect to the transaction at the time the cardholder first notifies the card issuer or the person honoring the credit card of that claim or defense. For the purpose of determining the amount of credit outstanding in the preceding sentence, payments and credits to the cardholder's account are deemed to have been applied, in the order indicated, to the payment of:

(i) Late charges in the order of their entry to the account;

(ii) Finance charges in order of their entry to the account, and

(iii) Debits to the account other than those set forth above, in the order in which each debit entry to the account was made.

1981, c. 243, § 25.

MASSACHUSETTS GENERAL LAWS ANNOTATED

266 § 37A CRIMES AND PUNISHMENTS

§ 37A. Misuse of credit cards; definitions

As used in sections thirty-seven A to thirty-seven C, inclusive, the following words shall have the following meanings, unless the context otherwise requires:

"Cardholder", the person named on the face of a credit card to whom or for whose benefit the credit card is issued by an issuer.

"Credit card", any instrument or device, whether known as a credit card, credit plate, or by any other name, issued with or without fee by an issuer for the use of the cardholder in obtaining money, goods, services or anything else of value on credit.

"Expired credit card", a credit card which is no longer valid because the term shown on its face has elapsed.

"Falsely embosses", completion of a credit card, without the authorization of the named issuer, by adding any of the matter, other than the signature of the cardholder, which an issuer requires to appear on the credit card before it can be used by a cardholder.

"Falsely makes", making or drawing, in whole or in part, a device or instrument which purports to be the credit card of a named issuer but which is not such a credit card because the issuer did not authorize the making or drawing, or altering a credit card which was validly issued.

"Incomplete credit card", a credit card that does not contain all of the matter that must be stamped, embossed, imprinted or written on said card other than the signature, as required by the issuer before it can be used by a cardholder.

"Issuer", the business organization or financial institution which issues a credit card or his duly authorized agent.

"Receives" or "receiving", acquiring possession or control or accepting as security for a loan.

"Revoked credit card", a credit card which is no longer valid because permission to use it has been suspended or terminated by the issuer.

§ 37B. Misuse of credit cards; penalties; multiple possession, presumption; arrest

Whoever, wih intent to defraud, *(a)* makes or causes to be made, either directly or indirectly, any false statement as to a material fact in writing, knowing it to be false and with intent that it be relied on, respecting his identity or that of any other person, or his financial condition or that of any other person, for the purpose of procuring the issuance of a credit card, or *(b)* takes a credit card from the person, possession, custody or control of another without the cardholder's consent by any conduct which would constitute larceny, or who, with knowledge that it has been so taken, receives the credit card with intent to use it or to sell it, or to transfer it to a person other than the issuer or cardholder, or *(c)* receives a credit card that he knows to have been lost, mislaid, or delivered under a mistake as to the identity or address of the cardholder, and who retains possession with intent to use it or to sell it or to transfer it to a person other than the issuer or the cardholder, or *(d)* being a person other than the issuer or his authorized agent, sells a credit card, or buys a credit card from a person other than the issuer or his authorized agent, or *(e)* being a person other than the cardholder or a person authorized by him, signs a credit card, or *(f)* uses, for the purpose of obtaining money, goods, services or anything else of value, a credit card obtained or retained in violation of clauses *(b)* to *(e),* inclusive, or a credit card which he knows is forged, expired or revoked, where the value of money, goods or services obtained in violation of this section is not in excess of one hundred dollars, or *(g)* obtains money, goods, services or anything else of value by representing without the consent of the cardholder that he is said cardholder or by representing that he is the holder of a card and such card has not in fact been issued, where the value of money, goods or services obtained is not in excess of one hundred dollars, or *(h)* being a person authorized by an issuer to furnish money, goods, services or anything else of value upon presentation of a credit card by the cardholder, or any agent or employees of such person, furnishes money, goods, services or anything else of value upon presentation of a credit card which he knows was obtained or retained in violation of clauses *(b)* to *(e)*, inclusive, or a credit card which he knows is forged, expired or revoked where the value of the goods or services obtained is not in excess of one hundred dollars, or *(i)* being a person who is authorized by an issuer to furnish money, goods, services or anything else of value upon presentation of a credit card by the cardholder, or any agent or employee of such person, fails to furnish money, goods, services or anything else of value which he represents in writing to the issuer that he has furnished, and the difference between the value of all money, goods, services and anything else of value actually furnished and the value represented to the issuer to have been furnished does not exceed one hundred dollars, or *(j)* receives money, goods, services or anything else of value obtained in violation of clauses *(f)* to *(i)*, inclusive or *(k)* makes a false statement in reporting a credit card to be lost or stolen, shall be punished by a fine of not more than five hundred dollars or by imprisonment in a jail or house of correction for not more than one year or both.

Whoever has in his possession or under his control stolen credit cards issued in the names of four or more other persons shall be presumed to have violated clause *(b)*.

Whoever is discovered by a police officer in the act of violating this section, while such officer is lawfully at or within the place where such violation occurs, may be arrested without a warrant by such police officer.

§ 37C. Fraudulent use of credit cards to obtain money, goods or services; false embossment of credit cards, multiple possession, presumption; arrest

Whoever, with intent to defraud, *(a)* obtains control over a credit card as security for debt, or *(b)* receives a credit card which he knows was taken or retained under circumstances which constitute credit card theft or a violation of clauses *(a)* or *(d)* of section thirty-seven B or clause *(a)* of this section, or *(c)* falsely makes or falsely embosses a purported credit card or utters such a credit card, or *(d)* obtains money, goods, services or anything else of value by use of a credit card obtained or retained in violation of clauses *(b)* to *(e),* inclusive, of section thirty-seven B, or by use of a credit card which he knows is forged, expired or revoked, where the value of the money, goods or services obtained in violation of this section is in excess of one hundred dollars, or *(e)* obtains money, goods or services or anything else of value by representing without the consent of the cardholder that he is said cardholder or by representing without the consent of the cardholder that he is said cardholder or by representing that he is the holder of a card and such card has not in fact been issued, where the value of money, goods or services obtained in violation of this section is in excess of one hundred dollars, or *(f)* being a person authorized by an issuer to furnish money, goods, services or anything else of value open presentation of a credit card which he knows was obtained in violation of subsections *(b)* to *(e)*, inclusive, of section thirty-seven B, or a credit card which he knows is forged, expired or revoked, when the value of the money, goods or services obtained is in excess of one hundred dollars, or *(g)* being a person authorized by an issuer to furnish money, goods, services or anything else of value upon presentation of a credit card by the services or anything else of value which he represents in writing to the issuer that he has furnished, and the difference between the value of all money, goods, services and anything else of value actually furnished and the value represented to the issuer to have been furnished exceeds one hundred dollars, or *(h)* receives money, goods, services or anything else of value obtained in violation of subsections *(f)* or *(g)* of section thirty-seven B, or *(i)* possesses one or more incomplete credit cards, intending to complete them without the consent of the issuer, or *(j)* possesses, with knowledge of its character, machinery, plates or any other contrivance designed to reproduce instruments purporting to be the credit cards of an issuer who has not consented to the preparation of such credit cards, shall be punished by a fine of not more than two thousand dollars, or by imprisonment in a jail or house of correction for not more than two and one half years or in the state prison for not more than five years, or by both such fine and imprisonment.

Whoever has in his possession or under his control four or more credit cards which are falsely embossed shall be presumed to have violated clause *(c)*.

Whoever is discovered by a police officer in the act of violating this section, while such officer is lawfully at or within the place where such violation occurs, may be arrested without a warrant by such police officer.

§ 37D. Credit card restrictions

Whoever publishes or causes to be published the number or code of an existing, canceled, revoked, expired, or nonexistent credit card issued by a public utility company or the numbering or coding system which is employed in the issuance of such credit cards, or any method, scheme, instruction or information on how to fraudulently avoid payment for telecommunication services, with the intent that such number or coding system or information be used or with knowledge that such system or information are to be used to fraudulently avoid the payment of any lawful charges imposed by a public utility company shall be punished by a fine not exceeding two thousand dollars or by imprisonment for not more than twelve months, or both.

As used in this section, "published" means the communication of information to any one or more persons, either orally, in person, or by telephone, radio, or television, or in a writing of any kind, including a letter or memorandum, circular, poster, or handbill, newspaper or magazine article, or book with the intent that such information be used or employed in violation of this section

Subtitle 14. Credit Card Number Protection Act.

§ 14-1401. Definitions.

(a) *In general.*—In this subtitle the following words have the meanings indicated.

(b) *Authorized use, disclosure, or receipt.*—"Authorized use, disclosure, or receipt" means any use, disclosure, or receipt necessary to accomplish the specific purpose for which the person issued a credit card number or payment device number granted to another the right to use, disclose, or receive the credit card number or other payment device number.

(c) *Payment device number.*—"Payment device number" means any code, account number, or other means of account access, other than a check, draft, or similar paper instrument, that can be used to obtain money, goods, services, or anything of value, or for purposes of initiating a transfer of funds. For purposes of § 14-1402 (a) (5) (iii) of this subtitle, this term does not include an encoded credit card number or encoded payment device number.

(d) *Holder.*—"Holder" means any person who:

(1) Has been issued a credit card number or other payment device number; or

(2) Is authorized by the person who has been issued a credit card number or other payment device number to use, disclose, or receive that credit card number or payment device number.

(e) *Person.*—"Person" includes an individual, corporation, business trust, estate, trust, partnership, association, two or more persons having a joint or common interest, or any other legal or commercial entity. (1984, chs. 747, 782.)

§ 14-1402. Protection of payment device numbers.

(a) *Who may disclose number.*—A person may not use or disclose any credit card number or other payment device number unless:

(1) The person is the holder of the credit card or payment device number;

(2) The disclosure is made to the holder or issuer of the credit card or payment device number;

(3) The use or disclosure is:

(i) Pursuant to obligations under federal or State law;

(ii) At the direction of a governmental entity pursuant to law; or

(iii) In response to the order of a court having jurisdiction to issue the order;

(4) Disclosure is in connection with an authorization, processing, billing, collection, chargeback, insurance collection, fraud prevention, or credit card or payment device recovery that relates to the credit card or payment device number, an account accessed by the credit card or payment account number, a debt for which the holder or person authorized by the holder gave the credit card number or payment device number for purposes of identification, or debts or obligations arising, alone or in conjunction with another means of payment, from the use of the credit card or payment device number;

(5) Except as provided in subsection (b) of this section, disclosure is reasonably necessary in connection with:

(i) The sale or pledge, or negotation of the sale or pledge, of any portion of a business or the assets of a business;

(ii) The management, operation, or other activities involving the internal functioning of the person making the disclosure; or

(iii) The management, operation, or other activities involving disclosures between a corporation and its subsidiaries or controlled affiliates or between the subsidiaries or the controlled affiliates, provided that a disclosure for marketing purposes may not be made if the holder of an active credit card or payment device number has notified the issuer in writing at an address specified by the issuer that such use is not permitted. The issuer shall provided holders of active accounts notice of such nondisclosure option and the specified address on a periodic basis at the issuer's discretion provided the time between such notifications does not exceed 1 year. The issuer shall comply with such elections within 45 days after receipt of the holder's response.

CHAPTER XXIVA. CREDIT CARDS

750.157m Definitions

Sec. 157m. As used in this chapter:

(a) "Credit card" means any instrument or device which is sold, issued or otherwise distributed by a business organization or financial institution for the use of the person or organization identified thereon for obtaining goods, property, services or anything of value on credit.

750.157n Stealing, removing, retaining or secreting another's card without consent

Sec. 157n. Any person who steals, knowingly takes or knowingly removes a credit card from the person or possession of a cardholder, or who knowingly retains or knowingly secretes a credit card without the consent of the cardholder, shall be guilty of a felony.

750.157p Possession of another's card with intent to circulate or sell

Sec. 157p. Any person who has in his possession, or under his control, or who receives from another person a credit card with the intent to circulate or sell the same, or to permit or cause or procure the same to be used, delivered, circulated or sold, knowing such possession, control or receipt to be without the consent of the cardholder, shall be guilty of a felony.

750.157q Delivery, circulation, or sale of wrongly held or obtained card

Sec. 157q. Any person who delivers, circulates or sells a credit card which was obtained or is held by such person under circumstances which would constitute an offense under sections 157n or 157p, or uses or permits or causes or procures the same to be used, delivered, circulated or sold, knowing the same to be obtained or held under circumstances which would constitute an offense under sections 157n or 157p, shall be guilty of a felony.

750.157r Fraud, forgery, material alteration; counterfeiting

Sec. 157r. Any person who, with intent to defraud, forges, materially alters or counterfeits a credit card, shall be guilty of a felony.

750.157s. Revoked or cancelled card, use with intent to defraud, notice, misdemeanor, punishment

Sec. 157s. Any person who, *for the purpose of obtaining goods, property, services or anything of value,* knowingly and with intent to defraud uses *** a credit card which has been revoked or canceled *** by the issuer thereof, as distinguished from expired, and notice of such revocation or cancellation has been received by such person through registered or certified mail or by personal service, shall be *guilty of a misdemeanor if the aggregate value of the goods, property, services or anything of value is $100.00 or less, and shall be guilty of a misdemeanor punishable by a fine of* not more than $1,000.00 or imprisoned not more than 1 year, or both, *if the aggregate value of the goods, property, services or anything of value is more than $100.00.*

750.157t Sales to or services performed for violators

Sec. 157t. Any person who sells or delivers goods or property or anything of value, or renders any service to any other person knowing that such other person has committed or is committing any act prohibited by this chapter shall be guilty of a felony.

750.157u Causing cardholder to be overcharged

Sec. 157u. Any person to whom a cardholder presents a credit card for the purpose of obtaining goods, property, services or anything of value on credit who, by forging or aiding in the forgery of the cardholder's signature or by filling out or completing a form supplied by the issuer of the credit card, causes the cardholder to be overcharged, shall be guilty of a felony.

MINNESOTA STATUTES ANNOTATED

FINANCIAL TRANSACTION CARDS

325G.02. Definitions

Subd. 2. "Financial transaction card" means an instrument or device, whether known as a credit card, credit plate, charge plate, courtesy card, bank services card, banking card, check guarantee card, debit card, or by any other name issued with or without fee by an issuer for the use of the holder to obtain credit, money, goods, services, or anything else of value, but does not mean a telephone company credit card.

Subd. 4. "Issuer" means a person or firm or its duly authorized agent, that issues a financial transaction card.

325G.03. Unsolicited financial transaction cards

No person in whose name a financial transaction card is issued shall be liable for any amount resulting from use of that card from which he or a member of his family or household derives no benefit unless he has accepted the card by (1) signing or using the card, or (2) authorizing the use of the card by another. A mere failure to destroy or return an unsolicited financial transaction card is not such an acceptance. Signing or using a card is not acceptance if those acts were performed under duress as defined under section 609.08.

325G.04. Lost or stolen financial transaction cards

Subdivision 1. No person in whose name a financial transaction card has been issued which he has accepted as provided in section 325G.03 shall be liable for any amount in excess of $50 resulting from the unauthorized use of the card from which he or a member of his family or household derives no benefit; provided, however, that the limitation on liability of this subdivision shall be effective only if the issuer is notified of any unauthorized charges contained in a bill within 60 days of receipt of the bill by the person in whose name the card is issued.

Subd. 2. No person in whose name a financial transaction card is issued shall be liable for any amount resulting from the unauthorized use of the financial transaction card after receipt by the issuer of notice that the card has been lost or stolen and from which such person or a member of his family or household derives no benefit.

325G.041. Married woman; name on card

If a financial transaction card issuer has determined in the normal course of business that it will issue a card to a married woman, the card shall be issued bearing either her current or former surname, as the woman may direct.

Financial transaction card issuers may require that a married woman requesting a card in a former surname open a new account in that name. Refusal to issue a financial transaction card pursuant to this section constitutes an unfair discriminatory practice under section 363.03, subdivision 8.

325G.05. Disputed accounts

Subdivision 1. Billing information. Every financial transaction card issuer shall include on each billing statement the name, address, and telephone number of the department designated by it to receive requests by the customer account holder to correct mistakes or make adjustments to the billing statement.

Subd. 2. Required response. Every financial transaction card issuer, within 30 days of receipt from a customer account holder, in writing at the address specified in subdivision 1, of a questioned or disputed charge, shall conduct an individual inquiry into the facts and send to the customer account holder an explanatory response in clear and definite terms.

Subd. 3. Violation. A violation of this section shall be treated as a violation of section 325F.69.

§ 97-19-5. Credit cards—title of law.

Sections 97-19-5 to 97-19-29 shall be known as the "Mississippi Credit Card Crime Law of 1968."

§ 97-19-9. Credit cards—definitions.

The following words and phrases as used in sections 97-19-5 to 97-19-29 shall have the following meanings ascribed to them, unless a different meaning is plainly required by the context:

(a) "Cardholder" is defined as the person or organization named on the face of a credit card, as defined hereinafter, to whom or for whose benefit the credit card is issued by an issuer.

(b) "Credit card" is defined as any instrument or device, whether known as a credit card, credit plate or by any other name, issued with or without fee by an issuer for the use of the cardholder or one authorized by him in obtaining money, goods, property, services or anything else of value on credit or in consideration of an undertaking or guaranty of the issuer of the payment of a check or draft drawn by the cardholder or one authorized by him.

(c) "Expired credit card" means a credit card which is no longer valid because the term shown on its face has elapsed.

(d) "Issuer" is defined as any business organization or financial institution, including but not limited to merchants, state and national banks, and any and all other persons, firms, corporations, trusts, and organizations, or any duly authorized agent thereof, which issues a credit card.

(e) "Receives" or "receiving" is defined as acquiring possession of or control of or accepting as security for a loan a credit card.

(f) "Revoked credit card" is defined as a credit card which is not longer valid because permission to use it has been suspended or terminated by the issuer.

(g) A credit card is "incomplete" if part of the matter other than the signature of the cardholder which an issuer requires to appear on the credit card before it can be used by a cardholder has not been stamped, embossed, imprinted or written on said card.

(h) A person "falsely makes" a credit card when he makes or draws in whole or in part a device or instrument which purports to be the credit card of a named issuer, but which is not in fact such a credit card because the issuer did not authorize the making or drawing of said card; or when one materially alters a credit card which was validly issued.

(i) A person "falsely embosses" a credit card when, without the authorization of the named issuer, he completes a credit card by adding any other matter than the signature of the cardholder which an issuer requires to appear on the credit card before it can be used by a cardholder.

§ 97-19-11. Credit cards—procuring issuance by false statements.

Any person who makes or causes to be made either directly or indirectly any false statement in writing with intent that it be relied upon with respect to his identity or that of any other person, firm or corporation, for the purpose of procuring the issuance of a credit card is guilty of a misdeamor.

§ 97-19-23. Credit cards—furnishing things of value on forged or unlawfully obtained card—failing to give value represented as given.

Any person or any agent of said person who is authorized to furnish money, goods, property, services, or anything else of value upon presentation of a credit card by the cardholder or one authorized by him, who, with intent to defraud the issuer, furnishes money, goods, property, services, or anything of value upon presentation of a credit card which he knows to have been obtained in violation of section 97-19-5 to 97-19-29 or a credit card which he knows to be forged, is considered to be in violation of said sections.

VERNON'S ANNOTATED MISSOURI STATUTES

§ 570.130. Fraudulent use of credit device

1. A person commits the crime of fraudulent use of a credit device if he uses a credit for the purpose of obtaining services or property, knowing that:

   (1) The device is stolen, fictitious or forged; or

   (2) The device has been revoked or cancelled; or

   (3) For any other reason his use of the device is unauthorized.

2. Fraudulent use of a credit device is a class A misdemeanor or unless the value of the property or services obtained or sought to be obtained within any thirty-day period is one hundred fifty dollars or more, in which case fraudulent use of a credit device in a class D felony.

REVISED STATUTES OF NEBRASKA

28-512. Theft by deception. A person commits theft if he obtains property of another by deception. A person deceives if he intentionally:

(4) Uses a credit card, charge plate, or any other insturment which purports to evidence after undertaking to pay for property or services delivered or rendered to or upon the order of a designated person or bearer (a) where such instrument has been stolen, forged, revoked, or canceled, or where for any other reason its use by the actor is unauthorized, or (b) where the actor does not have the intention and ability to meet all obligations to the issuer arising out of his use of the instrument.

The word deceive does not include falsity as to matters having no pecuniary signficance, or statements unlikely to deceive ordinary persons in the group address.

MONTANA CODE ANNOTATED

45-6-317. Deceptive practices.

(1) A person commits the offense of deceptive practices when he purposes or knowingly:

(i) using a credit card which was issued to another without the other's consent;

(ii) using a credit card that has been revoked or canceled;

(iii) using a credit card that has been falsely made, counterfeited, or altered in any material respect;

(iv) using the pretended number or description of a fictitous credit card;

(v) using a credit card which has expired provided the credit card clearly indicates the expiration date.

NEVADA REVISED STATUTES

CREDIT CARDS

205.610 Definitions.

As used in NRS 205.610 to 205.810, inclusive, unless the context otherwise requires, the words and terms defined in NRS 205.620 to 205.670, inclusive, have the meanings ascribed to them in those sections.

205.620 "Cardholder" defined.

"Cardholder" means the person or organization named on the face of a credit card to whom or for whose benefit the credit card is issued by an issuer.

205.630 "Credit card" defined.

"Credit card" means any instrument or device, whether known as a credit card, credit plate, or by any other name, issued with or without fee by an issuer for the use of the cardholder in obtaining money, property, goods, services or anything else of value on credit.

205.640 "Expired credit card"' defined.

"Issuer" means the business organization, financial institution or a duly authorized agent of a business organization or financial institution which issues a credit card.

205.660 "Receives" and "receiving" defined.

"Receives" or "receiving" means acquiring possession or control or accepting as security for a loan.

205.680 False statement to procure issuance of credit card.

Any person who, for the purpose of procuring the issuance of a credit card, makes or causes to be made, either directly or indirectly, any false statement in writing, knowing it to be false, with intent that it be relied on respecting his identity or financial condition or the identity or financial condition of any other person, firm or corporation is guilty of a gross misdemeanor.

205.690 Obtaining or possessing credit card without cardholder's consent; presumption from possession.

1. Any person who steals, takes or removes a credit card from a person, possession, custody or control of another without the cardholder's consent or who, with knowledge that a credit card has been so taken, removed or stolen receives the credit card with intent to circulate, use or sell it or to transfer it to a person other than the issuer or the cardholder, shall be punished by imprisonment in the state prison for not less than 1 year nor more than 6 years, or by a fine of not more than $5,000, or by both fine and imprisonment.

2. Any person who possesses a credit card without the consent of the cardholder and with the intent to circulate, use, sell or transfer the card with intent to defraud shall be punished by imprisonment in the state prison for not less than 1 year nor more than 6 years, or by a fine of not more than $5,000, or by both fine and imprisonment.

3. Any person who has in his possession or under his control two or more credit cards issued in the name of another person or persons is presumed to have obtained and to possess the credit cards with the knowledge that they have been stolen and with the intent to circulate, use, sell or transfer them with intent to defraud. The presumption established by this subsection does not apply to the possession of two or more credit cards

used in the regular course of the possessor's business or employment or where the possession is with the consent of the cardholder.

205.710 Sale or purchase of credit card of another.

Any person, except the issuer, who sells a credit card, or any person who buys a credit card from a person other than the issuer shall be punished by imprisonment in the state prison for not less than 1 year nor more than 6 years, or by a fine of not more than $5,000, or by both fine and imprisonment.

205.750 Unauthorized signing of credit card or related document with intent to defraud.

Any person, except the cardholder or a person authorized by the cardholder, who signs a credit card, sales slip, sales draft or instrument for the payment of money which evidences a credit card transaction with intent to defraud shall be punished by imprisonment in the state prison for not less than 1 year nor more than 10 years, or by a fine of not more than $10,000, or by both fine and imprisonment.

NEW HAMPSHIRE REVISED STATUTES ANNOTATED

638:5 Fraudulent Use of Credit Card.

I. A person is guilty of fraudulent use of a credit card if he uses a credit card for the purpose of obtaining property or services with knowledge that:
 (a) The card is stolen; or
 (b) The card has been revoked or cancelled; or
 (c) For any other reason his use of the card is unauthorized by either the issuer or the person to whom the credit card is issued.

II. "Credit card" means a writing or other evidence of an undertaking to pay for property or services delivered or rendered to or upon the order of a designated person or bearer.

III. Fraudulent use of a credit card is a class B felony if property or services are obtained which exceed the value of one hundred dollars. Any other violation of this section is a misdemeanor. The value may be determined according to the provisions of RSA 637:2, V, (a).

NEW JERSEY STATUTES ANNOTATED

2C:21-6. Credit Cards

a. **Definitions.** As used in this section:

(1) "Cardholder" means the person or organization named on the face of a credit card to whom or for whose benefit the credit card is issued by an issuer.

(2) "Credit card" means any instrument or device, whether known as a credit card, credit plate, or by any other name, issued with or without fee by an issuer for the use of the cardholder in obtaining money, goods, services or anything else of value on credit.

(3) "Expired credit card" means a credit card which is no longer valid because the term shown on it has elapsed.

(4) "Issuer" means the business organization or financial institution which issues a credit card or its duly authorized agent.

(5) "Receives" or "receiving" means acquiring possession or control or accepting a credit card as security for a loan.

(6) "Revoked credit card" means a credit card which is no longer valid because permission to use it has been suspended or terminated by the issuer.

b. **False statements made in procuring issuance of credit card.** A person who makes or causes to be made, either directly or indirectly, any false statement in writing, knowing it to be false and with intent that it be relied on, respecting his identity or that of any other person, firm or corporation, or his financial condition or that of any other person, firm or corporation, for the purpose of procuring the issuance of a credit card is guilty of a crime of the fourth degree.

c. **Credit card theft.**

(1) A person who takes a credit card from the person, possess, custody or control of another without the cardholder's consent or who, with knowledge that it has been so taken,

receives the credit card with intent to use it or to sell it, or to transfer it to a person other than the issuer or the cardholder is guilty of a crime of the fourth degree. Taking a credit card without consent includes obtaining it by any conduct defined and proscribed in Chapter 20 of this title, Theft and Related Offenses.

A person who has in his possession or under his control (a) credit cards issued in the names of two or more other persons *or, (b) two or more stolen credit cards* is presumed to have violated this paragraph.

(2) A person who receives a credit card that he knows to have been lost, mislaid, or delivered under a mistake as to the identity or address of the cardholder, and who retains possession with intent to use it or to sell it or to transfer it to a person other than the issuer or the cardholder is guilty of a crime of the fourth degree.

(3) A person other than the issuer who sells a credit card or a person who buys a credit card from a person other than the issuer is guilty of a crime of the fourth degree.

(4) A person who, with intent to defraud the issuer, a person or organization providing money, goods, services or anything else of value, or any other person.

(5) A person who, with intent to defraud a purported issuer, a person or organization providing money, goods, services or anything else of value, or any other person, falsely makes or falsely embosses a purported credit card or utters such a credit card is guilty of a third degree offense. A person other than the purported issuer who possesses two or more credit cards which are falsely made or falsely embossed is presumed to have violated this paragraph. A person "falsely makes; a credit card when he makes or draws, in whole or in part, a device or instrument which purports to be the credit card of a named issuer but which is not such a credit card because the issuer did not authorize the making or drawing, or alters a credit card which was validly issued. A person "falsely embosses" a credit card when, without the authorization of the named issuer, he completes a credit card by adding any of the matter, other than the signature of the cardholder, which an issuer requires to

appear on the credit card before it can be used by a cardholder.

(6) A person other than the cardholder or a person authorized by him who, with intent to defraud the issuer, or a person or organization providing money, goods, services or anything else of value, or any other person, signs a credit card, is guilty of a crime of the fourth degree. A person who possesses two or more credit cards which are so signed is presumed to have violated this paragraph.

d. Intent of cardholder to defraud; penalties; knowledge of revocation. A person, who, with intent to defraud the issuer, a person or organization providing money, goods, services or anything else of value, or any other person, (1) uses for the purpose of obtaining money, goods, services or anything else of value a credit card obtained or retained in violation of subsection c. of this section or a credit card which he knows is forged, expired or revoked, or (2) obtains money, goods, services or anything else of value by representing without the consent of the cardholder that he is the holder of a specified card or by representing that he is the holder of a card and such card has not in fact been issued, is guilty of a crime of the fourth degree. Knowledge of revocation shall be presumed to have been received by a cardholder four days after it has been mailed to him at the address set forth on the credit card or at his last known address by registered or certified mail, return receipt requested, and, if the address is more than 500 miles from the place of mailing, by air mail. If the address is located outside the United States, Puerto Rico, the Virgin Islands, the Canal Zone and Canada, notice shall be presumed to have been received 10 days after mailing by registered or certified mail.

e. Intent to defraud by person authorized to furnish money, goods, or services; penalties.

(1) A person who is authorized by an issuer to furnish money, goods, services or anything else of value upon presentation of a credit card by the cardholder, or any agent or employees of such person, who, with intent to defraud the issuer or the cardholder, furnishes money, goods, services or anything else of value upon presentation of a credit-card obtained or retained in violation of subsection c. of this section

or a credit card which he knows is forged, expired or revoked violates this paragraph and is guilty of a crime of the fourth degree.

(2) A person who is authorized by an issuer to furnish money, goods, services or anything else of value upon presentation of a credit card by the cardholder, fails to furnish money, goods, services or anything else of value which he represents in writing to the issuer that he has furnished is guilty of a crime of the fourth degree.

f. Incomplete credit cards; intent to complete without consent. A person other than the cardholder possessing 2 or more incomplete credit cards, with intent to complete them without the consent of the issuer or a person possessing, with knowledge of its character, machinery, plates or any other contrivance designed to reproduce instruments purporting to be the credit cards of an issuer who has not consented to the preparation of such credit cards, is guilty of a crime of the third degree. A credit card is "incomplete" if part of the matter other than the signature of the cardholder, which an issuer requires to appear on the credit card, before it can be used by a cardholder, has not yet been stamped, embossed, imprinted or written on it.

NEW MEXICO STATUTES ANNOTATED

30-16.25. Credit cards; definitions.

As used in Sections 30-16-25 through 30-16-38 NMSA 1978:

A. "cardholder" means the person or organization identified on the face of a credit card to whom or for whose benefit the credit card is issued by an issuer;

B. "credit card" means any instrument or device, whether known as a credit card, credit plate, charge card, or by any other name, issued with or without fee by an issuer for the use of the cardholder in obtaining money, goods, services or anything else of value, either on credit, or in consideration of an undertaking or guarantee by the issuer of the payment of a check drawn by the cardholder;

C. "expired credit card" means a credit card which shows on its face that it is outdated:

D. "issuer" means the business organization or financial institution, or its duly authorized agent, which issues a credit card;

E. "participating party" means a business organization, or financial institution, other than the issuer, which acquires for value a sales slip or agreement;

F. "sales slip or agreement" means any writing evidencing a credit card transaction;

G. "merchant" means every person who is authorized by an issuer or a participating party to furnish money, goods, services or anything else of value upon presentation of a credit card by a cardholder;

H. "incomplete credit card" means a credit card upon which a part of the matter, other than the signature of the cardholder, which an issuer requires to appear on the credit card before it can be used by a cardholder, has not been stamped, embossed, imprinted or written on it;

I. "revoked credit card" means a credit card for which the permission to use has been suspended or terminated by the issuer, and notice thereof has been given to the cardholder; and

J. "anything of value" includes money, goods and services.

30-16-25. Theft of a credit card by taking or retaining possession of card taken.

A person who takes a credit card from the person, possession, custody or control of another without the cardholder's consent, or who with knowledge that it has been so taken, acquires or possesses a credit card with the intent to use it or to sell it, or to transfer it to a person other than the issuer or the cardholder, is guilty of a fourth degree felony. Taking a credit card without consent includes obtaining it by conduct defined or known as statutory larceny, common-law larceny by trespassory taking, common-law larceny by trick, embezzlement or obtaining property by false pretense, false promise or extortion.

30-16-33. Fraudulent use of credit cards.

A. A person is guilty of a fourth degree felony if, with intent to defraud, he uses, to obtain anything of value:

(1) a credit card obtained in violation of Sections 30-16-25 through 30-16-25 through 30-16-38 NMSA 1978; or

(2) a credit card which is invalid, expired or revoked; or

(3) a credit card while fraudulently representing that he is the cardholder named on the credit card, or an authorized agent or representative of the cardholder named on the credit card; or

(4) a credit card issued in the name of another without the consent of the person to whom the card has been issued.

B. If the value of all things of value obtained by any person from one or more merchants, an issuer or a participating party, in violation of this section, exceeds three hundred dollars ($300) in any consecutive six months period, then the offense of the violator is a third degree felony.

McKINNEY'S CONSOLIDATED LAWS OF NEW YORK ANNOTATED

ARTICLE 29-A — CREDIT CARDS AND CREDIT IDENTIFICATION DEVICES

§ 511. Definitions

In this article, unless the context or subject matter otherwise requires:

1. "Credit card" means and includes any credit card, credit plate, charge plate, courtesy card, or other identification card or device issued by a person to another person which may be used to obtain a cash advance or a loan or credit or to purchase or lease property or services on the credit of the issuer or of the holder;

2. "Person" includes an individual, corporation, partnership or association, two or more persons have a joint or common interest or any other legal or commercial entity;

3. "Issuer" means a person who issues a credit card;

4. "Holder" means a person to whom such a credit card is issued or who has agreed with the issuer to pay obligations arising from the use of a credit card issued to another person;

5. "Unauthorized use" means use of a credit card by a person other than the holder who does not have actual, implied or apparent authority from the holder for such use and from which use the holder receives no benefit.

6. "Seller" means any person who honors credit cards which may be used to purchase or lease property or services on the credit of the issuer or of the holder.

7. "Lender" means any person who honors credit cards which may be used to obtain a cash advance or loan.

8. "Improper use" means unauthorized use of a credit card or use of a revoked, cancelled, expired or forged credit card at the premises of a seller or lender, to obtain a cash advance or loan, or to purchase or lease property or services on the credit of the issuer or holder, or to attempt to do so.

9. "Accepted credit card" means an accepted credit card as defined in the act of Congress entitled "Truth in Lending Act" and the regulations thereunder, as such act and regulations may from time to time be amended.

§ 512. Limitation of liability for unauthorized use of a credit card

1. A provision which imposes liability upon a holder for a cash advance or loan or for the purchase or lease of property or services obtained by the unauthorized use of a credit card shall not be enforceable to the extent that it imposes a greater liability upon the holder than is imposed under the provisions of the act of Congress entitled "Truth in Lending Act" and the regulations thereunder, as such act and regulations may from time to time be amended.

§ 514. Defenses

1. In any action for a cash advance or loan or for the purchase or lease of property or services through the use of a credit card, it shall be a defense that such obligation

(a) arose out of the unauthorized use of a credit card which was not delivered to the holder; or

(b) arose subsequent to the giving of notice by the holder

106

to the issuer of the unauthorized use, loss or theft, of such credit card; or

(c) is in excess of the limitation of liability provided in the act of Congress entitled "Truth in Lending Act" and the regulations thereunder, as such act and regulations may from time to time be amended.

2. If any of the defenses set forth in subdivision one of this section be established, the court shall order the issuer to pay the reasonable attorney's fees incurred in the defense of the action if the court finds

(a) that the holder has cooperated with the issuer in determining the facts and circumstances relating to such unauthorized use, loss or theft, of the credit card; and

(b) that notwithstanding such cooperation with the issuer, the issuer has brought the action without reasonable cause.

GENERAL STATUTES OF NORTH CAROLINA

ARTICLE 19B.

Financial Transaction Card Crime Act.

§ 14-113.8. Definitions.

The following words and phrases as used in this Chapter, unless a different meaning is plainly required by the context, shall have the following meanings:

(1) Automated Banking Device.—"Automated banking device" means any machine which when properly activated by a financial transaction card and/or personal identification code may be used for any of the purposes for which a financial transaction card may be used.

(2) Cardholder.—"Cardholder" means the person or organization named on the face of a financial transaction card to whom or for whose benefit the financial transaction card is issued by an issuer.

(3) Expired Financial Transaction Card.—"Expired financial transaction card" means a financial transaction card which is no longer valid because the term shown on it has elapsed.

(4) Financial Transaction Card.—"Financial transaction card" or "FTC" means any instrument or device whether known as a credit card, credit plate, bank services card, banking card, check guarantee card, debit card, or by any other name, issued with or without fee by an issuer for the use of the cardholder:

   a. In obtaining money, goods, services, or anything else of value on credit; or

   b. In certifying or guaranteeing to a person or business the availability to the cardholder of funds on deposit that are equal to or greater than the amount necessary to honor a draft or check payable to the order of such person or business; or

   c. In providing the cardholder access to a demand deposit account or time deposit account for the purpose of:

     1. Making deposits of money or checks therein; or

     2. Withdrawing funds in the form of money, money orders, or traveler's checks therefrom; or

     3. Transferring funds from any demand deposit account or time deposit account to any other demand deposit account or time deposit account; or

     4. Transferring funds from any demand deposit account or time deposit account to any credit card accounts, overdraft privilege accounts, loan accounts, or any other credit accounts in full or partial satisfaction of any outstanding balance owed existing therein; or

     5. For the purchase of goods, services or anything else of value; or

     6. Obtaining information pertaining to any demand deposit account or time deposit account;

   d. But shall not include a telephone number, credit number, or other credit device which is covered by the provisions of Article 19A of this Chapter.

(5) Issuer.—"Issuer" means the business organization or financial institution or its duly authorized agent which issues a financial transaction card.

(6) Personal Identification Code.—"Personal identification code" means a numeric and/or alphabetical code assigned to the cardholder of a financial transaction card by the issuer to permit authorized electronic use of that FTC.

(7) Presenting.—"Presenting" means, as used herein, those actions taken by a cardholder or any person to introduce a financial transaction card into an automated banking device, including utilization of a personal identification code, or merely displaying or showing a financial transaction card to the issuer, or to any person or organization providing money, goods, services, or anything else of value, or any other entity with intent to defraud.

(8) Receives.—"Receives" or "receiving" means acquiring possession or control or accepting a financial transaction card as security for a loan.

(9) Revoked Financial Transaction Card. — "Revoked financial transaction card" means a financial transaction card which is no longer valid because permission to use it has been suspended or terminated by the issuer.

NORTH DAKOTA CENTURY CODE ANNOTATED

CREDIT CARDS

51-14.1-01. Definition of credit cards and other terms and imposition of liability on cardholder.

In this chapter the following words and phrases shall, unless the context otherwise requires, have the following meanings:

1. "Accepted credit card" means any credit card which the cardholder has requested in writing or has signed or has used, or authorized another to use, for the purpose of obtaining money, property, labor, or services on credit. A renewal credit card shall be deemed to be accepted if it is issued within one year after a prior card has been paid for or used. A credit card issued in connection with a merger, acquisition, or the like of card issuers or credit card services in substitution for an accepted credit card shall be deemed to be an accepted credit card.

2. "Adequate notice" means a writing which is conspicuous and which is printed on the credit card or on each periodic statement.
3. "Card issuer" means any person who issues a credit card.
4. "Cardholder" means any person to whom a credit card is issued or any person who has agreed with the card issuer to pay obligations arising from the issuance of a credit card to another person.
5. "Conspicuous" means any term or clause which is so written that a reasonable person against whom it is to operate ought to have noticed it.
6. "Credit card" means any card, plate, coupon book, or other credit device existing for the purpose of obtaining money, property, labor, or services on credit.
7. "Unauthorized use" means a use of a credit card by a person other than the cardholder who does not have actual, implied, or apparent authority for such use and from which the cardholder receives no benefit.

MISUSE OF CREDIT CARDS

§ 2913.21 Misuse of credit cards.

(A) No person shall do any of the following:

(1) Practice deception for the purpose of procuring the issuance of a credit card, when a credit card is issued in actual reliance thereon;

(2) Knowingly buy or sell a credit card from or to a person other than the issuer.

(B) No person, with purpose to defraud, shall do any of the following:

(1) Obtain control over a credit card as security for a debt;

(2) Obtain property or services by the use of a credit card, in one or more transactions, knowing or having reasonable cause to believe that such card has expired or been revoked, or was obtained, is retained, or is being used in violation of law;

(3) Furnish property or services upon presentation of a credit card, knowing that such card is being used in violation of law;

(4) Represent or cause to be represented to the issuer of a credit card that property or services have been furnished, knowing that such representation is false.

(C) No person, with purpose to violate this section, shall receive, possess, control, or dispose of a credit card.

(D) Whoever violates this section is guilty of misuse of credit cards, a misdemeanor of the first degree. If the cumulative retail value of the property and services involved in one or more violations of division (B)(2), (3), or (4) of this section, which violations involve one or more credit card accounts and occur within a period of ninety consecutive days commencing on the date of the first violation, is one hundred fifty dollars or more, or if the offender has previously been convicted of a theft offense, then misuse of credit cards is a felony of the fourth degree.

§1550-1. Definitions

1. The term "credit card" means an identification card or device issued to a person, firm or corporation by a business organization which permits such person, firm or corporation to purchase or obtain goods, property or services on the credit of such organization.

2. "Debit card" means an identification card or device issued to a person, firm or corporation by a business organization which permits such person, firm or corporation to obtain access to or activate a consumer banking electronic facility.

§ 1550.2. Prohibitions on use of credit and debit cards- Penalties

Any person who knowingly uses or attempts to use in person or by telephone, for the purpose of obtaining credit, or for the purchase of goods, property or services, or for the purpose of obtaining cash advances in lieu of these items, or to deposit, obtain or transfer funds, either a credit card or a debit card which has not been issued to such person or which is not used with the consent of the person to whom issued or a credit card or a debit card which has been revoked or canceled by the issuer of such card and actual notice thereof has been given to such person, or a credit card or a debit card which is false, counterfeit or nonexistent is guilty of a misdemeanor and punishable by a fine of not more than One Hundred Dollars ($100.00) or imprisonment for not more than thirty (30) days or both such fine and imprisonment if the amount of the credit or purchase or funds deposited, obtained or transferred by such use does not exceed Fifty Dollars ($50.00); or by a fine of not less than One Hundred Dollars ($100.00) nor more than Five Hundred Dollars ($500.00) or imprisonment for not more than one (1) year or both such fine and imprisonment if the amount of the credit or purchase or funds deposited, obtained or transferred by such use exceeds Fifty Dollars ($50.00).

OKLAHOMA CREDIT CARD CRIME ACT OF 1970

§ 1550.21. Definitions

As used in this act:

(1) "Cardholder" means the person of organization named on the face of a credit card or debit card to whom or for whose benefit the credit card or debit card is issued.

(2) "Credit card" means any instrument or device, whether known as a credit card, credit plate, charge plate or by any other name, issued with or without fee by an issuer for the use of the cardholder in obtaining money, goods, services or anything else of value on credit and all such credit cards lawfully issued shall be considered the property of the cardholders or the issuer for all purposes.

(3) "Debit card" means any instrument or device, whether known as a debit card or by any other name, issued with or without fee by an issuer for the use of the cardholder in depositing, obtaining or transferring funds from a consumer banking electronic facility.

(4) "Issuer" means any person, firm, corporation, financial institution or its duly authorized agent which issues a credit card or a debit card.

(5) "Receives" or "receiving" means acquiring possession or control or accepting as security for a loan.

(6) "Revoked card" means a credit card or a debit card which is no longer valid because permission to use it has been suspended or terminated by the issuer.

§ 1550.22. Taking credit card or debit card—Receiving taken credit or debit card

(a) A person who takes a credit card or debit card from the person, possession, custody or control of another without the cardholder's consent, or who, with knowledge that it has been so taken, receives the credit card or debit card with intent to use it or to sell it, or to transfer it to a person other than the issuer or the cardholder, is guilty of card theft and is subject to the penalties set forth in Section 1550.33(a) of this title.

(b) Taking a credit card or a debit card without consent includes obtaining it by the crime of larceny, larceny by trick, larceny by the bailee, embezzlement or obtaining property by false pretense, false promise, extortion or in any manner taking without the consent of the cardholder or issuer.

(c) A person who has in his possession or under his control any credit card or debit card obtained under subsection (b) of this section is presumed to have violated this section.

§ 1550.23. Receiving, holding or concealing lost or mislaid card

A person who receives, holds or conceals a credit card or a debit card which has been lost or mislaid under circumstances which give him knowledge or cause to inquire as to the true owner and appropriates it to his use or the use of another not entitled thereto is subject to the penalties set forth in Section 1550.33(a) of Title 21 of the Oklahoma Statutes.

§ 1550.24. Selling or buying credit card or debit card

A person other than the issuer who sells a credit card or debit or a person who buys a credit card or a debit card from a person other than the issuer is guilty of theft and is subject to the penalties set forth in Section 1550.33(a) of this title.

§ 1550.25. Controlling credit or debit card as security for debt

A person with intent to defraud (a) the issuer, (b) a person or organization providing money, goods, services or anything else of value, or (c) any other person, who obtains control over a credit card or debit card as security for debt is guilty of theft and is subject to the penalties set forth in Section 1550.33(a) of this title.

§ 1550.26. Receiving taken or retained card upon giving consideration

A person, other than the issuer, who receives, on giving of any consideration, credit cards or debit cards issued to any other person, which he has reason to know were taken or retained under circumstances which constitute card theft, is guilty of card theft and is subject to the penalties set forth in Section 1550.33(a) of Title 21 of the Oklahoma Statutes.

§ 1550.27. False making or embossing of credit or debit card

(a) A person, with intent to defraud (1) a purported issuer, (2) a person or organization providing money, goods, services or anything else of value, or (3) any other person, who falsely makes or falsely embosses a purported credit card or debit card or utters such a credit card or debit card is guilty of forgery and is subject to the penalties set forth in Section 1550.33(a) of Title 21 of the Oklahoma Statutes.

(b) A person other than the purported issuer who possesses any credit card or debit card which is falsely made or falsely embossed is presumed to have violated this section.

(c) A person "falsely makes" a credit card or debit card when he makes or draws, in whole or in part, a device or instrument which purports to be the credit card or debit card of a named issuer but which is not such a credit card or debit card because the issuer did not authorize the making or drawing, or when he alters a credit card or debit card which was validly issued.

(d) A person "falsely embosses" a credit card or debit card when, without the authorization of the named issuer, he completed a credit card or debit card by adding any of the matter, other than the signature of the cardholder, which an issuer requires to appear on the credit card or debit card before it can be used by a cardholder.

OREGON REVISED STATUTES

165.055. Fraudulent use of a credit card.

(1) A person commits the crime of fraudulent use of a credit card if, with intent to injure or defraud, the person uses a credit card for the purpose of obtaining property or services with knowledge that:

(a) The card is stolen or forged; or

(b) The card has been revoked or canceled; or

(c) For any other reason the use of the card is unauthorized by either the issuer or the person to whom the credit card is issued.

(2) "Credit card" means a card, booklet, credit card number or other identifying symbol or instrument evidencing an undertaking to pay for property or services delivered or rendered to or upon the order of a designated person or bearer.

(3) Fraudulent use of a credit card is:

(a) A Class A misdemeanor if the aggregate total amount of property or services the person obtains or attempts to obtain is under $200.

(b) A Class C felony if the total amount of property or services the person obtains or attempts to obtain is $200 or more.

PERDON'S PENNSYLVANIA CONSOLIDATED STATUTES ANNOTATED

§ 4106. Credit cards

(a) **Offense defined.**—A person commits an offense if he:

(1) uses a credit card for the purpose of obtaining property or services with knowledge that:

    (i) the card is stolen, forged or fictitious;

    (ii) the card belongs to another person who has not

authorized its use;

(iii) the card has been revoked or canceled; or

(iv) for any other reason his use of the card is unauthorized by the issuer or the person to whom issued; or

(2) makes, sells, gives, or otherwise transfers to another, or offers or advertises, or aids and abets any other person to use a credit card with the knowledge or reason to believe that it will be used to obtain property or services without payment of the lawful charges therefor; or

(3) publishes a credit card or code of an existing, canceled, revoked, expired, or nonexistent credit card, or the numbering or coding which is employed in the issuance of credit cards, with knowledge or reason to believe that it will be used to avoid the payment for any property or services.

(b) Defenses.—It is a defense to prosecution under subparagraph (a)(1)(iv) of this section, if the actor proves by a preponderance of the evidence that he had the intent and ability to meet all obligations to the issuer arising out of his use of the card.

(c) Grading.—An offense under this section falls within the following classifications depending on the value of the property or service secured or sought to be secured by means of the credit card;

(1) if the value involved exceeds $500, the offense constitutes a felony of the third degree; or

(2) if the value involved was $50 or more but less than $500, the offense constitutes a misdemeanor of the second degree; or

(3) if the value involved was less than $50, the offense constitutes a summary offense.

Amounts involved in unlawful use of a credit card pursuant to one scheme or course of conduct, whether from the same issuers or several issuers, may be aggregated in determining the classification of the offense.

(d) Definitions.—As used in this section the following words and phrases shall have the meanings given to them in this subsection:

"**Credit card.**" A writing or number or other evidence of an undertaking to pay for property or services delivered or rendered to or upon the order of a designated person or bearer.

"**Publishes.**" The communication of information to any one or more persons, either orally in person, or by telephone, radio or television or in a writing of any kind, including without limitation a letter or memorandum, circular or handbill, newspaper or magazine article, or book.

(e) **Venue.**—Any offense committed under (a) (1) of this section may be deemed to have been committed at either the place where the attempt to obtain property or services is made, or at the place where the property or services were received or provided, or at the place where the lawful charges for said property or services are billed.

GENERAL LAWS OF RHODE ISLAND

CHAPTER 49
CREDIT CARD CRIME ACT

11-49-1. Definitions.—As used in this chapter:

(A) "Cardholder" means the person or organization named on the face of a credit card to whom or for whose benefit the credit card is issued by an issuer.

(B) "Credit card" means any instrument or device, whether known as a credit card, credit plate or by any other name, issued with or without fee by an issuer for the use of the card holder in obtaining money, goods, services or anything else of value on credit.

(C) "Expired credit card" means a credit card which is no longer valid because the term shown on it has elapsed.

(D) "Issuer" means the business organization or financial institution, or its duly authorized agent, which issues a credit card.

(E) "Receives" or "receiving" means acquiring possession or control or accepting as security for a loan a credit card.

(F) "Revoked credit card" means a credit card which is no longer valid because permission to use it has been suspended or terminated by the issuer.

11-49-4. Fraudulent use of credit cards.—

A person who, with intent to defraud the issuer or a person or organization providing money, goods, services or anything else of value or any other person, uses, for the purpose of obtaining money, goods, services or anything else of value, a credit card obtained or retained in violation of this law or a credit card which he knows is forged, expired or revoked or who obtains money, goods, services or anything else of value by representing, without the consent of the cardholder, that he is the holder of a specified card or by representing that he is the holder of a card and such card has not in fact been issued, violates this subsection and is subject to the penalties set forth in subsection (1) of § 11-49-10, if the value of all moneys, goods, services and other things of value obtained in violation of this subsection does not exceed one hundred dollars ($100) in any six (6) month period. The violator is subject to the penalties set forth in subsection (2) of § 11-49-10, if such value does exceed one hundred dollars ($100) in any six (6) month period. Knowledge of revocation shall be presumed to have been received by a cardholder four (4) days after it has been mailed to him at the address set forth on the credit card or at his last known address by registered or certified mail, return receipt requested, and, if the address is more than five hundred (500) miles from the place of mailing, by air mail. If the address is located outside the United States, Puerto Rico, the Virgin Islands, the Canal Zone or Canada, notice shall be presumed to have been received ten (10) days after mailing by registered or certified mail

CODE LAWS OF SOUTH CAROLINA

CHAPTER 14

Financial Transaction Card Crime Act

§ 16-14-10. Definitions.

The following words and phrases as used in this chapter, unless a different meaning is plainly required by the context, shall have the following meanings:

(1) "Automated banking device" means any machine which when properly activated by a financial transaction card or personal identification code may be used for any of the purposes for which a financial transaction card may be used.

(2) "Cardholder" means the person or organization named on the face of a financial transaction card to whom or for whose benefit the financial transaction card is issued by an issuer.

(3) "Expired financial transaction card" means a financial transaction card which is no longer valid because the term shown on it has elapsed.

(4) "Financial transaction card" or "FTC" means any instrument or device whether known as a credit card, credit plate, bank services card, banking card, check guarantee card, debit card, or by any other name, issued with or without fee by an issuer for the use of the cardholder;

    (a) in obtaining money, goods, services, or anything else of value on credit;

    (b) in certifying or guaranteeing to a person or business the availability to the cardholder of funds on deposit that are equal to or greater than the amount necessary to honor a draft or check payable to the order of such person or business;

    (c) in providing the cardholder access to a demand deposit account or time deposit account for the purpose of:

        1. making deposits of money or checks therein;

        2. withdrawing funds in the form of money, money orders, or traveler's checks therefrom;

        3. transferring funds from any demand deposit account or time deposit account to any other demand deposit account or time deposit account;

        4. transferring funds from any demand deposit account or time deposit account to any credit card accounts, overdraft privilege accounts, loan accounts, or any other credit accounts in full or partial satisfaction of any outstanding balance owed existing therein;

5. for the purchase of goods, services or anything else of value;
6. obtaining information pertaining to any demand deposit account or time deposit account.

(5) "issuer" means the business organization or financial institution or its duly authorized agent which issues a financial transaction card.

(6) "Personal identification code" means a numeric or alphabetical code assigned to the cardholder of a financial transaction card by the issuer to permit authorized electronic use of that FTC.

(7) "Presenting" means those actions taken by a cardholder or any person to introduce a financial transaction card into an automated banking device, including utilization of a personal identification code, or merely displaying or showing a financial transaction card to the issuer, or to any person or organization providing money, goods, services, or anything else of value, or any other entity with intent to defraud.

(8) "Receives" or "receiving" means acquiring possession or control or accepting a financial transaction card as security for a loan.

(9) "Revoked financial transaction card" means a financial transaction card which is no longer valid because permission to use it has been suspended or terminated by the issuer.

§ 16-14-70. Criminal possession of financial transaction card forgery devices.

(a) A person is guilty of criminal possession of financial transaction card forgery devices when:

(1) he is a person other than the cardholder and possesses two or more incomplete financial transaction cards, with intent to complete them without the consent of the issuer;

(2) he possesses, with knowledge of its character, machinery, plates, or any other contrivance designed to reproduce instruments purporting to be financial transaction cards of an issuer who has not consented to the preparation of such financial transaction cards.

76-6-506. Financial transaction card offenses — Definitions.

For purposes of this part:

(1) "Automated banking device" means any machine which, when properly activated by a financial transaction card or a personal identification code, may be used for any of the purposes for which a financial transaction card may be used.

(2) "Card holder" means any person or organization named on the face of a financial transaction card to whom or for whose benefit a financial transaction card is issued by an issuer.

(3) "Financial transaction card" means:

(a) Any credit card, credit plate, bank services card, banking card, check guarantee card, debit card, telephone credit card, or any other card, issued by an issuer for the use of the card holder in obtaining money, goods, services, or anything else of value on credit, or in certifying or guaranteeing to a person or business the availability to the card holder of the funds on deposit that are equal to or greater than the amount necessary to honor a draft or check payable to the order of the person or business; or

(b) Any instrument or device used in providing the card holder access to a demand or time deposit account for the purpose of making deposits of money or checks in the account, or withdrawing funds from the account in the form of money, money orders, travelers' checks or other form representing value, or transferring funds from any demand or time deposit account to any credit card account in full or partial satisfaction of any outstanding balance existing in the credit card account.

(4) "Issuer" means a business organization or financial institution or its agent that issues a financial transaction card.

(5) "Personal identification code" means any numerical or alphabetical code assigned to a card holder by the issuer to permit the authorized electronic use of his financial transaction card.

CHAPTER 105.

Credit Cards

§ 4041. Definitions

As used in this chapter:

(1) As used herein, the term "person" shall include a natural person, a firm, an association and a corporation, and any officer, employee or agent thereof.

(2) "Cardholder" means any person to whom a credit card is issued and any person who has agreed with the card issuer to pay obligations arising from the issuance of a credit card to another person.

(3) "Card issuer" means any person who issues a credit card.

(4) "Credit card" means any instrument, whether known as credit card, credit plate, charge plate, or any other name, which purports to evidence an undertaking to pay for property, labor or services paid, delivered or rendered to or upon the order of persons designated or otherwise authorized as bearers of such card, and includes bank credit cards as defined in section 1301(b) of Title 8.

(5) "Accepted credit card" means any credit card which the cardholder has signed or has used, or authorized another to use, for the purpose of obtaining money, property, labor, or services on credit, and also the term includes a credit card issued in replacement or renewal of an accepted credit card.

(6) "Unauthorized use" means a use of a credit card to obtain money, property, labor or services by a person other than the cardholder who does not have actual, implied or apparent authority for such use.

(7) "Notice of loss instructions" shall be a separate slip or card, or a provision clearly printed in bold type in a cardholder agreement or accompanying material which shall apprise cardholder of the potential liability for unauthorized use, shall designate the address and telephone number of an office or offices of issuer to which adequate notice of loss may be given and which shall contain a blank space for the cardholder to

insert his account number, which space shall be identified to invite such insertion.

(8) "Adequate notice of loss" shall be an actual notice of loss or theft or of unauthorized use of the card to a designated office of issuer which may be by mail, telephone, telegraph, or in person.—

§ 4042. Liability for unauthorized use

A provision imposing liability on a cardholder for the unauthorized use of a credit card shall be effective only if the card is an accepted credit card, the liability imposed is not in excess of one hundred dollars, the cardholder has received notice of loss instructions from issuer, and the unauthorized use occurs before the cardholder has given adequate notice of loss to issuer.—

§ 4043. Fraudulent use

A person shall not with intent to defraud, obtain, or attempt to obtain money, property, services or any other thing of value, by the use of a credit card which he knows, or reasonably shall have known, to have been stolen, forged, revoked, cancelled, unauthorized or invalid for use by him for such purpose.—

§ 4044. Penalty

(a) A person who violates section 4043 of this title shall be fined not more than $500.00 or be imprisoned not more than 6 months, or both, if the aggregate value of the money, property, services or other things of value so obtained is $500.00 or less.

(b) A person who violates section 4043 of this title shall be fined not more than $1,000.00 or be imprisoned not more than one year, or both, if the aggregate value of the money, property, services or other things of value so obtained exceeds $50.00.—

SUBCHAPTER C. CREDIT

§ 32.31. Credit Card Abuse

(a) For purposes of this section:

(1) "Cardholder" means the person named on the face of a credit card to whom or for whose benefit the credit card is issued.

(2) "Credit Card" means an identification card, plate, coupon, book, number, or any other device authorizing a designated person or bearer to obtain property or services on credit. It includes the number or description of the device if the device itself is not produced at the time of ordering or obtaining the property or service.

(3) "Expired credit card" means a credit card bearing an expiration date after that date has passed.

(b) A person commits an offense if:

(1) with intent to obtain property or service fraudulently, he presents or uses a credit card with knowledge that:

(A) the card, whether or not expired, has not been issued to him and is not used with the effective consent of the cardholder; or

(B) the card has expired or has been revoked or cancelled;

(2) with intent to obtain property or service, he uses a fictitious credit card or the pretended number or description of a fictitious credit card;

(3) he receives property or service that he knows has been obtained in violation of this section;

(4) he steals a credit card or, with knowledge that it has been stolen, receives a credit card with intent to use it, to sell it, or to transfer it to a person other than the issuer or the cardholder;

(5) he buys a credit card from a person who he knows is not the issuer;

(b) A financial transaction card is incomplete if part of the matter other than the signature of the cardholder, which an issuer requires to appear on the financial transaction card before it can be used by a cardholder, has not yet been stamped, embossed, imprinted, encoded or written upon it.

Conviction of criminal possession of financial transaction card forgery devices is punishable as provided in § 16-14-100(b).

SOUTH DAKOTA CODIFIED LAWS

CHAPTER 54-11

CREDIT CARDS AND REVOLVING CHARGE ACCOUNTS

54-11-1. "Credit card" defined.

The term "credit card" as used in §§ 54-11-3 and 54-11-4, means an identification card or device issued by a business organization authorizing the person or entity to whom issued to purchase or obtain goods, property or services on credit.

54-11-3. Notice of cancellation or revocation of credit card.

For purposes of this chapter notice of the cancellation or revocation of a credit card may be given either by telegraph or in writing by certified mail. In the absence of proof of earlier delivery notice in writing by certified mail directed to the person to whom the card was issued at the address shown on the card or the last-known address, if deposited postpaid in the United States mail, shall be prima facie evidence that it was given on the second day after the date it was deposited. However, in lieu of such certified letter, a telegram addressed to the person to whom the card was issued at the address shown on the card or the last known post-office address of such person, if sent and filed in the office of a telegraph company serving the address locality, shall be prima facie evidence that it was given two days after it was filed.

39-3-501. Short title.—

Sections 39-3-501—39-3-513 shall be known and may be cited as the "State Credit Card Crime Act." [Acts 1969, ch. 121, § 1;

39-3-502. Definitions.—

As used in §§ 39-3-501 — 39-3-513 unless the context requires otherwise, words and terms shall have the following meanings:

39-3-502. Definitions.—

As used in §§39-3-501 — 39-3-513 unless the context requires otherwise, words and terms shall have the following meanings:

(a) "Cardholder" means the person or organization named on the face of a credit card to whom or for whose benefit the credit card is issued by an issuer.

(b) "Credit card" means any instrument or device, whether known, as a credit card, credit plate, credit number, charge plate, or by any other name, issued with or without fee by an issuer for the use of the cardholder in obtaining money, goods, services, or anything else of value on credit.

(c) "Credit card theft" means taking a credit card without consent and includes obtaining it by conduct defined or known as statutory larceny, common-law larceny by trespassory taking, common-law larceny by trick, embezzlement, or obtaining property by false pretense, false promise or extortion.

(d) "Expired credit card" means a credit card which is no longer valid because the term shown on it has expired.

(e) "Falsely makes" means a person who makes or draws, in whole or in part, a device or instrument which purports to be the credit card of a named issuer but which is not such a credit card because the issuer did not authorize the making or drawing, or alters a credit card which was validly issued.

(f) "Falsely embossess" means a person who, without the authorization of the named issuer, completes a credit card by adding any of the matter, other than the signature of the cardholder, which an issuer requires to appear on the credit card before it can be used by a cardholder.

(g) "Incomplete credit card" means a part of the matter other than the signature of the cardholder, which an issuer requires to appear on the credit card, before it can be used by a cardholder, has not yet been stamped, embossed, imprinted or written on it.

(h) "Issuer" means the business organization or financial institution which issues a credit card or its duly authorized agent.

(i) "Receives" or "receiving" means acquiring possession or control or accepting as security for a loan.

(j) "Revoked credit card" means a credit card which is no longer valid because permission to use it has been suspended or terminated by the issuer.

39-3-503. Making of false statements to procure issuance of a credit card. —

A person who makes or causes to be made, either directly or indirectly, any false statement in writing, knowing it to be false and with intent that it be relied on, respecting his identity or that of any other person, firm, or corporation, or his financial condition or that of any other person, firm, or corporation, for the purpose of procuring the issuance of a credit card, violates this section and is subject to the penalties set forth in subsection (a) of § 39-3-510.

39-3-504. Credit card theft and forgery — Receiving, selling or buying credit cards or information. —

(a) A person who takes a credit card or the information therefrom from the person, possession, custody or control of another without the cardholder's consent or who, with knowledge that it has been so taken, receives the credit card or the information with intent to use it or to sell it, or to transfer it to a person other than the issuer or the cardholder is guilty of credit card theft and is subject to the penalties set forth in subsection (a) of § 39-3-510. A person who has in his possession

123

or under his control credit cards issued in the names of two (2) or more other persons, without their knowledge and consent, is presumed to have violated this subsection.

(b) A person who receives a credit card that he knows to have been lost, mislaid, or delivered under a mistake as to the identity or address of the cardholder, and who retains possession with intent to use it or to sell it or to transfer it to a person other than the issuer or the cardholder is guilty of credit card theft and is subject to the penalties set forth in subsection (a) of § 39-3-510.

(c) A person other than the issuer who sells a credit card or a person who buys a credit card from a person other than the issuer violates this subsection and is subject to the penalties set forth in subsection (a) of § 39-3-510.

(d) A person, who with intent to defraud the issuer, a person, or organization providing money, goods, services, or anything else of value, or any other person, obtains control over a credit card as security for debt violates this subsection and is subject to the penalties set forth in subsection (a) of § 39-3-510.

(e) A person, other than the issuer, who during any twelve (12) month period, receives credit cards issued in the names of two (2) or more persons which he knows were taken or retained under circumstances which constitute credit card theft or a violation of § 39-3-503 or subsection (c) or (d) of this section violates this subsection and is subject to the penalties set forth in subsection (b) of § 39-3-510.

(f) A person who, with intent to defraud a purported issuer, a person or organization providing money, goods, services or anything else of value, or any other person, falsely makes or falsely embosses a purported credit card or utters such a credit card is guilty of credit card forgery and is subject to the penalties set forth in subsection (b) of § 39-3-510.

(g) A person other than the cardholder or a person authorized by him who, with intent to defraud the issuer, or a person or organization providing money, goods, services or anything else of value, or any other person, signs a credit card, violates this subsection and is subject to the penalties set forth in subsection (a) of § 39-3-510.

76-6-506. Financial transaction card offenses — Definitions.

For purposes of this part:

(1) "Automated banking device" means any machine which, when properly activated by a financial transaction card or a personal identification code, may be used for any of the purposes for which a financial transaction card may be used.

(2) "Card holder" means any person or organization named on the face of a financial transaction card to whom or for whose benefit a financial transaction card is issued by an issuer.

(3) "Financial transaction card" means:

(a) Any credit card, credit plate, bank services card, banking card, check guarantee card, debit card, telephone credit card, or any other card, issued by an issuer for the use of the card holder in obtaining money, goods, services, or anything else of value on credit, or in certifying or guaranteeing to a person or business the availability to the card holder of the funds on deposit that are equal to or greater than the amount necessary to honor a draft or check payable to the order of the person or business; or

(b) Any instrument or device used in providing the card holder access to a demand or time deposit account for the purpose of making deposits of money or checks in the account, or withdrawing funds from the account in the form of money, money orders, travelers' checks or other form representing value, or transferring funds from any demand or time deposit account to any credit card account in full or partial satisfaction of any outstanding balance existing in the credit card account.

(4) "Issuer" means a business organization or financial institution or its agent that issues a financial transaction card.

(5) "Personal identification code" means any numerical or alphabetical code assigned to a card holder by the issuer to permit the authorized electronic use of his financial transaction card.

CHAPTER 105.

Credit Cards

§ 4041. Definitions

As used in this chapter:

(1) As used herein, the term "person" shall include a natural person, a firm, an association and a corporation, and any officer, employee or agent thereof.

(2) "Cardholder" means any person to whom a credit card is issued and any person who has agreed with the card issuer to pay obligations arising from the issuance of a credit card to another person.

(3) "Card issuer" means any person who issues a credit card.

(4) "Credit card" means any instrument, whether known as credit card, credit plate, charge plate, or any other name, which purports to evidence an undertaking to pay for property, labor or services paid, delivered or rendered to or upon the order of persons designated or otherwise authorized as bearers of such card, and includes bank credit cards as defined in section 1301(b) of Title 8.

(5) "Accepted credit card" means any credit card which the cardholder has signed or has used, or authorized another to use, for the purpose of obtaining money, property, labor, or services on credit, and also the term includes a credit card issued in replacement or renewal of an accepted credit card.

(6) "Unauthorized use" means a use of a credit card to obtain money, property, labor or services by a person other than the cardholder who does not have actual, implied or apparent authority for such use.

(7) "Notice of loss instructions" shall be a separate slip or card, or a provision clearly printed in bold type in a cardholder agreement or accompanying material which shall apprise cardholder of the potential liability for unauthorized use, shall designate the address and telephone number of an office or offices of issuer to which adequate notice of loss may be given and which shall contain a blank space for the cardholder to

insert his account number, which space shall be identified to invite such insertion.

(8) "Adequate notice of loss" shall be an actual notice of loss or theft or of unauthorized use of the card to a designated office of issuer which may be by mail, telephone, telegraph, or in person.—

§ 4042. Liability for unauthorized use

A provision imposing liability on a cardholder for the unauthorized use of a credit card shall be effective only if the card is an accepted credit card, the liability imposed is not in excess of one hundred dollars, the cardholder has received notice of loss instructions from issuer, and the unauthorized use occurs before the cardholder has given adequate notice of loss to issuer.—

§ 4043. Fraudulent use

A person shall not with intent to defraud, obtain, or attempt to obtain money, property, services or any other thing of value, by the use of a credit card which he knows, or reasonably shall have known, to have been stolen, forged, revoked, cancelled, unauthorized or invalid for use by him for such purpose.—

§ 4044. Penalty

(a) A person who violates section 4043 of this title shall be fined not more than $500.00 or be imprisoned not more than 6 months, or both, if the aggregate value of the money, property, services or other things of value so obtained is $500.00 or less.

(b) A person who violates section 4043 of this title shall be fined not more than $1,000.00 or be imprisoned not more than one year, or both, if the aggregate value of the money, property, services or other things of value so obtained exceeds $50.00.—

SUBCHAPTER C. CREDIT

§ 32.31. Credit Card Abuse

(a) For purposes of this section:

(1) "Cardholder" means the person named on the face of a credit card to whom or for whose benefit the credit card is issued.

(2) "Credit Card" means an identification card, plate, coupon, book, number, or any other device authorizing a designated person or bearer to obtain property or services on credit. It includes the number or description of the device if the device itself is not produced at the time of ordering or obtaining the property or service.

(3) "Expired credit card" means a credit card bearing an expiration date after that date has passed.

(b) A person commits an offense if:

(1) with intent to obtain property or service fraudulently, he presents or uses a credit card with knowledge that:

(A) the card, whether or not expired, has not been issued to him and is not used with the effective consent of the cardholder; or

(B) the card has expired or has been revoked or cancelled;

(2) with intent to obtain property or service, he uses a fictitious credit card or the pretended number or description of a fictitious credit card;

(3) he receives property or service that he knows has been obtained in violation of this section;

(4) he steals a credit card or, with knowledge that it has been stolen, receives a credit card with intent to use it, to sell it, or to transfer it to a person other than the issuer or the cardholder;

(5) he buys a credit card from a person who he knows is not the issuer;

(6) not being the issuer, he sells a credit card;

(7) he uses or induces the cardholder to use the cardholder's credit card to obtain property or service for the actor's benefit for which the cardholder is financially unable to pay;

(8) not being the cardholder, and without the effective consent of the cardholder, he signs or writes his name or the name of another on a credit card with intent to use it;

(9) he possesses two or more incomplete credit cards that have not been issued to him with intent to complete them without the effective consent of the issuer. For purposes of the subdivision, a credit card is incomplete if part of the matter that an issuer requires to appear on the credit card before it can be used (other than the signature of the cardholder) has not yet been stamped, embossed, imprinted, or written on it;

(10) being authorized by an issuer to furnish goods or services on presentation of a credit card, he, with intent to defraud the issuer or the cardholder, furnishes goods or services on presentation of a credit card obtained or retained in violation of this section or a credit card that is forged, expired, or revoked; or

(11) being authorized by an issuer to furnish goods or services on presentation of a credit card, he, with intent to defraud the issuer or a cardholder, fails to furnish goods or services that he represents in writing to the issuer that he has furnished.

(c) It is presumed that a person who used a revoked, cancelled, or expired credit card had knowledge that the card had been revoked, cancelled, or expired if he had received notice of revocation, cancellation, or expiration from the issuer. For the purposes of this section, notice may be either notice given orally in person or by telephone, or in writing by mail or by telegram. If written notice was sent by registered or certified mail with return receipt requested, or by telegram with report of delivery requested, addressed to the cardholder at the last address shown by the records of the issuer, it is presumed that the notice was received by the cardholder no later than five days after sent.

(d) An offense under this section is a felony of the third degree.

CODE OF VIRGINIA

ARTICLE 6.

Offenses Relating to Credit Cards.

§ 18.2-191. Definitions. —

The following words and phrases as used in this article, unless a different meaning is plainly required by the context, shall have the following meanings:

"Cardholder" means the person or organization named on the face of a credit card to whom or for whose benefit the credit card is issued by an issuer.

"Credit card" means any instrument or device, whether known as a credit card, credit plate, payment device number, or by any other name, issued with or without fee by an issuer for the use of the cardholder in obtaining money, goods, services or anything else of value on credit. For the purpose of this article, "credit card" shall also include a similar device, whether known as a debit card, or any other name, issued with or without fee by an issuer for the use of the cardholder in obtaining money, goods, services or anything else of value by charging the account of the cardholder with a bank or any other person even though no credit is thereby extended.

"Expired credit card" means a credit card which is no longer valid because the term shown on it has elapsed.

"Issuer" means the business organization or financial institution or its duly authorized agent which issues a credit card.

"Payment device number" means any code, account number or other means of account access, other than a check, draft or similar paper instrument, that can be used to obtain money, goods, services or anything else of value, or to initiate a transfer of funds. "Payment device number" does not include an encoded or truncated credit card number or payment device number.

130

"Receives" or *"receiving"* means acquiring possession or control of the credit card number or payment device number or accepting the same as security for a loan.

"Revoked credit card" means a credit card which is no longer valid because permission to use it has been suspended or terminated by the issuer.

"Sales draft" means a paper form evidencing a purchase of goods, services or anything else of value from a merchant through the use of a credit card.

"Cash advance/withdrawal draft" means a paper form evidencing a cash advance or withdrawal from a bank or other financial institution through the use of a credit card.

§ 18.2-192. Credit card theft.—

(1) A person is guilty of credit card or credit card number theft when:

(a) He takes, obtains or withholds a credit card or credit card number from the person, possession, custody or control of another without the cardholder's consent or who, with knowledge that it has been so taken, obtained or withheld, receives the credit card or credit card number with intent to use it or sell it, or to transfer it to a person other than the issuer or the cardholder; or

(b) He receives a credit card or credit card number that he knows to have been lost, mislaid, or delivered under a mistake as to the identity or address of the cardholder, and who retains possession with intent to use, to sell or to transfer the credit card or credit card number to a person other than the issuer or the cardholder; or

(c) He, not being the issuer, sells a credit card or credit card number or buys a credit card or credit card number from a person other than the issuer; or

(d) He, not being the issuer, during any twelve-month period, receives credit cards or credit card numbers issued in the names of two or more persons which he has reason to know were taken or retained under circumstances which constitute a violation of § 18.2-95.

§ 18.2-193. Credit card forgery.—

(1) A person is guilty of credit card forgery when:

(a) With intent to defraud a purported issuer, a person or organization providing money, goods, services or anything else of value, or any other person, he falsely makes or falsely embosses a purported credit card or utters such a credit card; or

(b) He, not being the cardholder or a person authorized by him, with intent to defraud the issuer, or a person or organization providing money, goods, services or anything else of value, or any other person, signs a credit card; or

(c) He, not being the cardholder or a person authorized by him, with intent to defraud the issuer, or a person or organization providing money, goods, services or anything else or value, or any other person, forges a sales draft or cash advance/withdrawal draft, or uses a credit card number of a card of which he is not the cardholder, or utters, or attempts to employ as true, such forged draft knowing it to be forged.

(2) A person falsely makes a credit card when he makes or draws, in whole or in part, a device or instrument which purports to be the credit card of a named issuer but which is not such a credit card because the issuer did not authorize the making or drawing, or alters a credit card which was validly issued.

REVISED CODE OF WASHINGTON ANNOTATED

9A.56.140 Possessing stolen property—Definition—Credit cards, presumption.

(1) "Possessing stolen property" means knowingly to receive, retain, possess, conceal, or dispose of stolen property knowing that it has been stolen and to withhold or appropriate the same to the use of any person other than the true owner or person entitled thereto.

(2) The fact that the person who stole the property has not been convicted, apprehended, or identified is not a defense to a charge of possessing stolen property.

(3) When a person not an issuer or agent thereof has in his

possession or under his control stolen credit cards issued in the names of two or more persons, he shall be presumed to know that they are stolen. This presumption may be rebutted by evidence raising a reasonable inference that the possession of such stolen credit cards was without knowledge that they were stolen.

WEST VIRGINIA CODE

§ 61-3-24a. Obtaining or attempting to obtain goods, property or service by false or fraudulent use of credit cards or other false or fraudulent means; penalties.

It shall be unlawful for any person knowingly to obtain or attempt to obtain credit, or to purchase or attempt to purchase any goods, property or service, by the use of any false, fictitious or counterfeit credit card, telephone number, credit number or other credit device, or by the use of any credit card, telephone number, credit number or other credit device of another beyond or without the authority of the person to whom such card, number or device was issued, or by the use of any credit card, telephone number, credit number or other credit device in any case where such card, number or device has been revoked and notice of revocation has been given to the person to whom issued.

It shall be unlawful for any person knowingly to obtain or attempt to obtain, by the use of any fraudulent scheme, device, means or method, telephone or telegraph service or the transmission of a message, signal or other communication by telephone or telegraph, or over telephone or telegraph facilities with intent to avoid payment of charges therefor.

The word "notice" as used in the first paragraph of this section shall be construed to include either notice given in person or notice given in writing to the person to whom the number, card or device was issued. The sending of a notice in writing by registered or certified mail in the United States mail, duly stamped and addressed to such person at his last known address, shall be prima facie evidence that such notice was duly received.

Any person who violates any provision of this section shall, if the credit, goods, property, service or transmission be of the value of one hundred dollars or more, be deemed guilty of a felony, and, upon conviction thereof, shall be punished by imprisonment in the penitentiary not less than one nor more than ten years; and if of less value, be deemed guilty of a misdemeanor, and, upon conviction thereof, shall be punished by imprisonment in jail not exceeding one year or by a fine of not more than five hundred dollars, or, in the discretion of the court, by both such imprisonment and fine. Any person convicted of an attempt to commit an offense under the provisions of this section shall be guilty of a misdemeanor, and, upon conviction thereof, shall be punished by imprisonment in jail not exceeding six months or by a fine of not more than three hundred dollars, or, in the discretion of the court, by both such imprisonment and fine.

WISCONSIN CODE ANNOTATED

943.41. Financial transaction card crimes

(1) Definitions.—In this section:

(a) "Alter" means add information to, change information on or delete information from.

(am) "Automated financial service facility" means a machine activated by a financial transaction card, personal identification code or both.

(b) "Cardholder" means the person * * * to whom or for whose benefit * * * *a financial transaction* card is issued * * *

(c) "Counterfeit" means to manufacture, produce or create by any means a * * * *financial transaction* card or purported * ** *financial transaction* card without the issuer's consent or authorization.

(d) Repealed by L.1981, c. 288, § 5, eff. May 1, 1982.

(e) "Expired credit card" means a * * * *financial transaction* card which is no longer valid because the term shown thereon has elapsed.

(em) "Financial transaction card" means an instrument or

device issued by an issuer for the use of the cardholder in any of the following:

1 Obtaining anything on credit.

2. Certifying or guaranteeing the availability of funds sufficient to honor a draft or check.

3. Gaining access to an account.

(f) "Issuer" means the business organization or financial institution which issues a * * * *financial transaction* card or its duly authorized agent.

(fm) "Personal identification code" means a numeric, alphabetic, alphanumeric code or other means of identification required by an issuer to permit a cardholder's authorized use of a financial transaction card.

* * * * * * *

(h) "Revoked * * * *financial transaction* card" means a * * * *financial transaction* card which is no longer valid because permission to use it has been suspended or terminated by the issuer.

(2) **False statements.** No person shall make or cause to be made, whether directly or indirectly, any false statements in writing, knowing it to be false and with intent that it be relied upon, respecting his identity or that of any other person or his financial condition or that of any other person or other entity for the purpose of procuring the issuance of a * * * *financial transaction* card.

(3) **Theft by taking card.** (a) No person shall acquire a * * * *financial transaction* card from the person, possession, custody or control of another without the cardholder's consent, or, with knowledge that it has been so acquired, receive the * * * *financial transaction* card with intent to use it or sell it or to transfer it to a person other than the issuer. Acquiring a * * * *financial transaction* card without consent includes obtaining it by conduct defined as statutory theft. If a person has in his possession or under his control * * * *financial transaction* cards issued in the names of 2 or more other persons it is prima facie evidence that he acquired them in violation of this subsection.

(b) No person shall receive a * * * *financial transaction* card that he knows to have been lost, mislaid, or delivered under a mistake as to the identity or address of the cardholder, and retain possession thereof with intent to sell it, or to transfer it to a person other than the issuer or the cardholder, or to use it. The possession of such a * * * *financial transaction* card for more than 7 days by a person other than the issuer or the cardholder is prima facie evidence that such person intended to sell, transfer or use it in violation of this subsection.

(c) No person other than the issuer shall sell a * * * *financial transaction* card. No person shall buy a * * * *financial transaction* card from a person other than the issuer.

(d) No person shall, with intent to defraud the issuer, a person or organization providing money, goods, services or anything else of value, or any other person, obtain control over a * * * *financial transaction* card as security for debt.

(e) No person * * * other than the issuer * * * *may* receive * * * *a financial transaction card* issued in the * * * *name of another person* which he *or she* has reason to know * * * *was* taken or retained * * * *in violation of* this subsection or sub. (2). *Either of the following is prima facie evidence of a violation of this paragraph:*

1. Possession of 3 or more financial transaction cards with reason to know that the financial transaction cards were taken or retained in violation of this subsection or sub. (2).

2. Possession of a financial transaction card with knowledge that the financial transaction card was taken or retained in violation of this subsection or sub. (2).

(4) Forgery of financial transaction card. (a) No person shall, with intent to defraud a purported issuer, a person or organization providing money, goods, services or anything else of value or any other person, alter or counterfeit a * * * *financial transaction* card or purported * * * *financial transaction* card or possess a * * * *financial transaction* card or purported * * * *financial transaction* card with knowledge that it has been altered or counterfeited. The possession by a person other than the purported issuer of 2 or more * * * *financial transaction* cards which have been altered or counterfeited is prima facie evidence that the person intended to defraud or that he knew the * * * *financial transaction* cards to have been so altered or counterfeited.

(b) No person other than the cardholder or a person authorized by him shall, with intent to defraud the issuer, a person or organization providing money, goods, services or anything else of value or any other person, sign a * * * *financial transaction* card. Possession by a person other than the intended cardholder or one authorized by the intended cardholder of a * * * *financial transaction* card signed by such person is prima facie evidence that such person intended to defraud in violation of this subsection.

(5) Fraudulent use. (a) No person shall, with intent to defraud the issuer, a person or organization providing money, goods, services or anything else of value or any other person, 1) use for the purpose of obtaining money, goods, services or anything else of value, a * * * *financial transaction* card obtained or retained in violation of sub. (3) or a * * * *financial transaction* card which he knows is forged, expired or revoked, or 2) obtain money, goods, services or anything else of value by representing without the consent of the cardholder that he is the holder of a specified card or by representing that he is the holder of a card and such card has not in fact been issued. Knowledge of revocation shall be presumed to have been received by a cardholder 4 days after it has been mailed to him at the address set forth on the * * * *financial transaction* card or at his last-known address by registered or certified mail, return receipt requested, and if the address is more than 500 miles from the place of mailing, by air mail. If the address is located outside the United State, Puerto Rico, the Virgin Islands, the Canal Zone and Canada, notice shall be presumed to have been received 10 days after mailing by registered or certified mail.

(b) No cardholder shall use a * * * *financial transaction* card issued to him or allow another person to use a * * * *financial transaction* card issued to him with intent to defraud the issuer, a person or organization providing money, goods, services or anything else of value or any other person.

(c) No person may deposit a stolen or forged instrument by

means of an automated financial service facility with knowledge of the character of the instrument.

(d) No person may, with intent to defraud anyone:

(1) Introduce information into an electronic funds transfer system.

(2) Transmit information to or intercept or alter information from an automated financial service facility.

(e) No person may knowingly receive anything of value from a violation of par. (c) or (d).

(6) Fraudulent use; other persons. (a) No person who is authorized by an issuer to furnish money, goods, services or anything else of value upon presentation of a * * * *financial transaction* card by the cardholder, or any agent or employee of such person, shall, with intent to defraud the issuer or the cardholder, furnish money, goods, services or anything else of value upon presentation of a * * * *financial transaction* card obtained or retained under circumstances prohibited by sub. (3) or a * * * *financial transaction* card which he knows is forged, expired or revoked.

(b) No person who is authorized by an issuer to furnish money, goods, services or anything else of value upon presentation of a * * * *financial transaction* card by the cardholder, or any agent or employee of such person, shall, with intent to defraud, fail to furnish money, goods, services or anything else of value which he represents in writing to the issuer that he has furnished.

(c) No person other than the cardholder shall possess an incomplete * * * *financial transaction* card with intent to complete it without the consent of the issuer. A * * * *financial transaction* card is "incomplete" if part of the matter, other than the signature of the cardholder, which an issuer requires to appear on the * * * *financial transaction* card before it can be used by a cardholder has not yet been stamped, embossed, imprinted or written on it.

FEDERAL LEGISLATION
SELECTED PROVISIONS: CHAPTER 41-
CONSUMERS CREDIT PROTECTION ACT

TITLE 15—COMMERCE AND TRADE

§ 1642. Issuance of credit cards

No credit card shall be issued except in response to a request or application therefor. This prohibition does not apply to the issuance of a credit card in renewal of, or in substitution for, an accepted credit card.

EFFECTIVE DATE

Section 503(1) of Pub. L. 91-508 provided that: "Section 132 of such Act [this section] takes effect upon the date of enactment of this title [Oct. 26, 1970]."

SECTION REFERRED TO IN OTHER SECTIONS

This section is referred to in section 1645 of this title.

§ 1643. Liability of holder of credit card

(a) Limits on liability

(1) A cardholder shall be liable for the unauthorized use of a credit card only if:

    (A) the card is an accepted credit card;

    (B) the liability is not in excess of $50;

    (C) the card issuer gives adequate notice to the cardholder of the potential liability;

    (D) the card issuer has provided the cardholder with a description of a means by which the card issuer may be notified of loss or theft of the card, which description may be provided on the face or reverse side of the statement required by section 1637(b) of this title or on a separate notice accompanying such statement;

(E) the unauthorized use occurs before the card issuer has been notified that an unauthorized use of the credit card has occurred or may occur as the result of loss, theft, or otherwise; and

(F) the card issuer has provided a method whereby the user of such card can be identified as the person authorized to use it.

(2) For purposes of this section, a card issuer has been notified when such steps as may be reasonably required in the ordinary course of business to provide the card issuer with the pertinent information have been taken, whether or not any particular officer, employee, or agent of the card issuer does in fact receive such information.

(b) Burden of proof

In any action by a card issuer to enforce liability for the use of a credit card, the burden of proof is upon the card issuer to show that the use was authorized or, if the use was unauthorized, then the burden of proof is upon the card issuer to show that the conditions of liability for the unauthorized use of a credit card, as set forth in subsection (a) of this section, have been met.

(c) Liability imposed by other laws or by agreement with issuer

Nothing in this section imposes liability upon a cardholder for the unauthorized use of a credit card in excess of his liability for such use under other applicable law or under any agreement with the card issuer.

(d) Exclusiveness of liability

Except as provided in this section, a cardholder incurs no liability from the unauthorized use of a credit card.

SECTION REFERRED TO IN OTHER SECTIONS

This section referred to in sections 1602, 1645 of this title.

§ 1644. Fraudulent use of credit cards; penalties

(a) Use, attempt or conspiracy to use card in transaction affecting interstate or foreign commerce

Whoever knowingly in a transaction affecting interstate or foreign commerce, uses or attempts or conspires to use any counterfeit, fictitious, altered, forged, lost, stolen, or fraudulently obtained credit card to obtain money, goods, services, or anything else of value which within any one-year period has a value aggregating $1,000 or more; or

(b) Transporting, attempting or conspiring to transport card in interstate commerce

Whoever, with unlawful or fraudulent intent, transports or attempts or conspires to transport in interstate or foreign commerce a counterfeit, fictitious, altered, forged, lost, stolen, or fraudulently obtained credit card knowing the same to be counterfeit, fictitious, altered, forged, lost, stolen, or fraudulently obtained; or

(c) Use of interstate commerce to sell or transport card

Whoever, with unlawful or fraudulent intent, uses any instrumentality of interstate or foreign commerce to sell or transport a counterfeit, fictitious, altered, forged, lost, stolen, or fraudulently obtained credit card knowing the same to be counterfeit, fictitious, altered, forged, lost, stolen, or fraudulently obtained; or

(d) Receipt, concealment, etc., of goods obtained by use of card

Whoever knowingly receives, conceals, uses, or transports money, goods, services, or anything else of value (except tickets for interstate or foreign transportation) which (1) within any one-year period has a value aggregating $1,000 or more, (2) has moved in or is part of, or which constitutes interstate or foreign commerce, and (3) has been obtained with a counterfeit, fictitious, altered, forged, lost, stolen, or fraudulently obtained credit card; or

141

(e) Receipt, concealment, etc., of tickets for interstate or foreign transportation obtained by use of card

Whoever knowingly receives, conceals, uses, sells, or transports in interstate or foreign commerce one or more tickets for interstate or foreign transportation, which (1) within any one-year period have a value aggregating $500 or more, and (2) have been purchased or obtained with one or more counterfeit, fictitious, altered, forged, lost, stolen, or fraudulently obtained credit cards; or

(f) Furnishing of money, etc., through use of card

Whoever in a transaction affecting interstate or foreign commerce furnishes money, property, services, or anything else of value, which within any one-year period has a value aggregating $1,000 or more, through the use of any counterfeit, fictitious, altered, forged, lost, stolen, or fraudulently obtained credit card knowing the same to be counterfeit, fictitious, altered, forged, lost, stolen, or fraudulently obtained—
shall be fined not more than $10,000 or imprisoned not more than ten yars, or both.

MODEL PENAL CODE
American Law Institute

§ 224.6 Credit Cards

A person commits an offense if he uses a credit card for the purpose of obtaining property or services with knowledge that:

    (1) the card is stolen or forged; or

    (2) the card has been revoked or cancelled; or

    (3) for any other reason his use of the card is unauthorized by the issuer.

It is an affirmative defense to prosecution under paragraph (3) if the actor proves by a preponderance of the evidence that he had the purpose and ability to meet all obligations to the issuer arising out of his use of the card. "Credit card" means a writing or other evidence of an undertaking to pay for property or services delivered or rendered to or upon the order of a designated person or bearer. An offense under this Section is a felony of the third degree if the value of the property or services secured or sought to be secured by means of the credit card exceeds $500; otherwise it is a misdemeanor.

Appendix D
YOUR J.C. PENNEY RETAIL INSTALLMENT
CREDIT AGREEMENT
(Revolving Credit Agreement)

In this agreement, *you* and *your* mean everyone who signs the agreement or is bound by it. *We, us,* and *our* means J.C. Penney Company, Inc., 1301 Avenue of the Americas, New York, NY 10019.

Credit Reports — Before we open an account, we may check the information you have given us with credit bureaus or with others. We may also request additional information from them, including a credit report, before approving your application. We may ask for a credit report after your account is opened if we want to update our records, renew your account, or decide whether to give you additional credit. If you ask, we will tell you if we requested a credit report. If so, we will give you the name and address of the credit bureau that supplied the report.

Types of Charges — There are two types of charges under a J.C. Penney account: regular charges and major purchase charges. Any merchandise or service may be purchased from us and billed as a regular charge. Certain types of merchandise identified in our stores and catalogs may be billed as major purchase charges.

Promise to Pay — You must pay for all purchases charged to your account by you or an authorized user or from which you receive a benefit.

Billing Statements — If you have a balance on your account, we will send you a monthly statement. It will state the minimum amount you must pay be the "payment due date" to keep your account current.

145

Finance Charge — Finance charge not in excess of that permitted by law will be assessed on the outstanding balance(s) from month to month. You do not pay any finance charge if there is no previous balance, or if credits and payments made within 25 days of the current "Billing Date" equal or exceed the balance at the beginning of the period.

The finance charge is based on your regular and major purchase "average daily balance" during the period. Here's how we find your average daily balance:

(1) We take the beginning balance of your account each day, including any unpaid finance charge from a previous billing period, and subtract any insurance premiums, returned check fees, and late charges.

(2) We subtract any payments as of the day we receive them and any credits as of the date we issue them. We add any new purchases as of the date they were made. (We do not add new purchases in New Mexico.) This gives us the daily balance.

(3) Then, we add up all the daily balances for the billing cycle and divide the total by the number of days in the billing cycle. This gives us the "average daily balance."

If you have a regular charge balance and a major purchase balance, we figure the average daily balance for each. Then we combine them to determine your finance charge by applying to the combined average daily balance the current periodic rate of 1.75% (*annual percentage rate* 21%). If you have only a regular charge balance, there is a minimum **finance charge** of 50¢. There is no minimum finance charge if you live in the District of Columbia or if you have only a major purchase balance.

Payment Requirements—You can pay your entire balance at any time. Or you can pay any amount from the minimum payment due, to the entire balance. The larger the payment that you make on your entire balance, and the sooner we receive your payment, the less finance charge you will have to pay.

Failure to Pay — If you do not pay on time, we can require that you make immediate payment of your entire balance, subject to any rights you have by state law to correct your non-payment. We may use an outside attorney to collect your account.

If there is a lawsuit and you lose, you agree to pay reasonable attorney's fees, plus court costs, as permitted by the law in your state.

Late Payment Charge — This applies to you if you live in AZ, GA, KY, MD, NV, NH, OR, SD, TN, VA, or outside the U.S. If we do not receive your required payment within two consecutive billing periods, we will assess a late payment charge. This charge is 5% of the late payment (excluding any insurance premiums and returned check fees), but not more than $5.00.

Returned Check FEE — As permitted by law, if any check sent to us as payment on your account and/or for insurance premiums is returned unpaid by your bank, we will charge you a reasonable returned check fee.

Our Rights — We can change our credit terms at any time. We will notify you in advance of any such changes as required by law. Our new terms may be applied to the existing balance on your account unless prohibited by law. We can limit or cancel your credit privileges. All J.C. Penney charge cards belong to us and you must return them at our request.

We give up any rights to any mechanic's or materialman's liens on real property used or expected to be used as your principal residence. If you live in Florida, we will keep a security interest in any items charged to your account, except for those items that are considered real property under state law.

If you Move — You must notify us promptly if you move. If your new residence is in another state, our terms in that state will apply only to purchases you make after we receive notice of your move. If you move outside the U.S. (50 states), our standard charge account terms will apply.

Your Account Information — We may give information about how you have handled your account to credit bureaus or others who may lawfully receive such information. We may also give or obtain information from others when: you have not paid on time; it is necessary to handle your account properly; we think there is a question of illegal or improper activity; we receive a legitimate request from a governmental authority; or we are required to do so by law.

We may use information about you for other business purposes. This includes sharing information about you with other companies that are part of the J.C. Penney family.

Advertisements in the Mail — Because many customers like to shop at home, we send advertisements with billing statements and in separate mailings. These advertisements may be for sale events, special interests items, offerings from J.C. Penny catalogs or insurance companies, among other things. If you do not want to receive these advertisements, you can tell us at the credit desk in any J.C. Penney store, or you can write to the credit office address shown on your billing statement.

Your required payment may include any amount past due from a previous month and any late charge or returned check fee. If you have an insurance policy that is billed with your J.C. Penney account, your minimum payment will include the amount of any premiums due that month.

Regular Charges — When there's a regular charge balance, you must make at least minimum payment each month.

IF YOUR REGULAR THEN YOUR MINIMUM
CHARGE BALANCE IS: MONTHLY PAYMENT IS:

$ 15.00 or less Balance	
15.01—100	$15
100.01—200	20
200.01—250	25
250.01—300	30
300.01—350	35
350.01—400	40
400.01—450	45
450.01—500	50
Over $500 1/10 Balance	

Major Purchase Charges — When there's a major purchase balance, you will pay at least a fixed amount each month. This amount is based on your highest major purchase balance in any month. Even if you reduce your balance, your monthly payment will still be based on that highest balance, as long as an unpaid balance remains. Payments over the required monthly amount will reduce by this amount the payment that will be required the following months(s).

IF YOUR HIGHEST MAJOR THEN YOUR
PURCHASE BALANCE IS: MONTHLY PAYMENT IS:

$200.01—210	$ 9.00
210.01—225	9.50
225.01—240	10.00
240.01—225	10.50

For balances between $255.01 and $375, the monthly payment is increased by 50¢ for each additional $15 or less.

$375.01—405	$15.00
405.01—420	15.50
420.01—435	16.00
435.01—450	16.50
450.01—465	17.00
465.01—495	17.50
495.01—510	17.75
510.01—525	18.25

For balances over $525, the monthly payment is increased by 50¢ for each additional $15 or less.

The law requires us to give you the following notices.

NOTICE: See reverse side for important information regarding your rights to dispute billing errors.

NOTICE: ANY HOLDER OF THIS CONSUMER CREDIT CONTRACT IS SUBJECT TO ALL CLAIMS AND DEFENSES WHICH THE DEBTOR COULD ASSERT AGAINST THE SELLER OF GOODS OR SERVICES OBTAINED PURSUANT HERETO OR WITH THE PROCEEDS HEREOF, RECOVERY HEREUNDER BY THE DEBTOR SHALL NOT EXCEED AMOUNTS PAID BY THE DEBTOR HEREUNDER.

The Ohio laws against discrimination require that all creditors make credit equally available to all creditworthy customers, and that credit reporting agencies maintain separate credit histories on each individual upon request. The Ohio Civil Rights Commission administers compliance with this law.

NOTICE TO THE BUYER: Do not sign this credit agreement before your read it or if it contains any blank spaces. You are entitled to a completely filled in copy of the credit agreement when you sign it. Keep it to protect your legal rights. You have the right to pay in advance the full amount due.

Maryland: Our charge account program for Maryland customers is subject to the provisions of Subtitle 9 of Title 12 of the Commercial Law Article of the Maryland code.

J.C. Penney Company, Inc.

Ted L. Spurlock
Vice President
Director of Credit and Consumer Banking Services

JCPenney Charge Application

YOUR SIGNATURE(S) MEAN(S) THAT YOU HAVE READ, UNDERSTOOD, AND AGREE TO THE TERMS OF THE ABOVE RETAIL INSTALLMENT CREDIT AGREEMENT.

Applicant's Signature	Date	Co-Applicant's Signature	Date

General Information — (Please Print All Information)

			FOR OFFICE USE ONLY
Type of Account You Want (Check One) ☐ Individual ☐ Joint	Have You Applied For A JCPenney Account Before? Applicant ☐ Yes ☐ No Where When	Co-Applicant ☐ Yes ☐ No Where When	DATE
Name Of Applicant To Whom Our Billing Statements Should Be Sent (First, Initial, Last)	Social Security Number	Date Of Birth / /	No. Of Dependent Children	TB
Name of Co-Applicant , if Joint Account Requested (First, Initial, Last)	Social Security Number	Date Of Birth / /	Relationship To Applicant	ID
Name And Relationship(s) To Applicant(s) Of Any Other Person(s) You Will Allow To Charge Purchases To Your Account (First, Initial, Last)			CCA

Information About Applicant To Whom Our Billing Statements Should Be Sent

				CCAB
Present Residence — Street	Apt.	City, State	Zip	DATE
Area Code & Phone Number ( )	How Long At This Address Yrs. Mos.	Monthly Mtge./Rent	DO YOU: ☐ Own ☐ Rent ☐ Own Mobile Home ☐ Live With Parents ☐ Other (Please Specify)	CCID
Former Address (if current residence less than two years) - Street	Apt.	City, State	Zip	How Long

Additional Information About Applicant / Information About Co-Applicant (if joint account requested)

Employer (Give Firm's Full Name)		How Long	Employer (Give Firm's Full Name)		How Long
Employer's Address (Street/City/State)		Business Telephone ( )	Employer's Address (Street/City/State)		Business Telephone ( )
Type Of Business	Monthly Salary	Present Position	Type Of Business	Monthly Salary	Present Position

You Need Not Furnish Alimony, Child Support Or Separate Maintenance Income Information If You Do Not Want Us To Consider It In Evaluating Your Application

Other Income — Source(s)	Amount (Monthly)	Other Income — Source(s)	Amount (Monthly)

Bank Accounts (Include Co-Applicant's, If Joint Account Requested)

Bank — Branch 1.	Account In The Name Of	Account Number	Checking & Savings Checking Savings Loan
Bank — Branch 2.	Account In The Name Of	Account Number	Checking & Savings Checking Savings Loan

Credit References (Include Co-Applicant's, If Joint Account Requested)   Credit Cards (Include Loan Or Finance Companies)

Firm Name	Location	Account/Loan Number	Account/Loan In The Name Of
1.			
2.			
3.			

Personal References

Name Of Nearest Relative Not Living At Address of Applicant Or Co-Applicant	Relationship To Applicant	Present Residence Address (Street/City/State)	Area Code & Phone Number ( )

JCP-9500 (Rev. 9/85)   After completing application, detach at perforation, fold down from top, moisten flap, fold and seal. Postage paid by JCPenney

152

INDEX